PORTO TRAVEL GUIDE

2025

Unveiling the Charm of Portugal's Second City

Jeffrey M. Martin

Copyright © Jeffrey M. Martin

All rights reserved. No part of this publication may be reproduced, distributed, or transmitted in any form or by any means, including photocopying, recording, or other electronic or mechanical methods, without the prior written permission of the publisher, except in the case of brief quotations embodied in critical reviews and certain other noncommercial uses permitted by copyright law

Table of contents

Introductions	**6**
History and Significance.	13
When to Visit.	16
Getting to Porto.	19
One Week Itinerary	21
Practical Information	24
Navigating the City	**27**
Transport Options	27
Public Transportation Guide	30
Walking Tours.	32
Biking in Porto.	34
Safety Tips	37
Must-see Attractions	**40**
Ribeira District.	40
Livraria Lello.	43
Dom Luís I Bridge	45
Porto Cathedral	47
Wine Cellars in Vila Nova de Gaia.	50
São Bento Train Station	53
Palácio de Bolsa	55
Market of Bolhão.	58
Casa de Música	61
Jardim do Morro.	63
Culinary Delights.	**66**
Traditional Dishes To Try	66

Top Restaurants and Cafes	69
Local Markets and Food Tours.	71
Wine Tasting Experiences	74
Street Food Guide	76
Cultural Experiences	**79**
Festivals & Events	79
Museums & Galleries	82
Music and Nightlife	85
Art & Architecture	88
Local Customs and Etiquette	91
Outdoor Adventures.	**93**
Parks and Greenspaces	93
River Activities	96
Day Trips from Porto.	100
Shopping in Porto.	**106**
Souvenir Ideas	106
Local Markets.	109
Boutique and Artisan Shops	112
Best Shopping Streets	115
Online Shopping Tips	118
Accommodation Options	**121**
Types of Accommodations	121
The Best Neighborhoods to Stay	**124**
Budget versus Luxury Stays	126
Booking Tips	129
Unique Places to Stay	133
Understanding Local Laws and Customs	**136**
Essential Legal Information	136

Health and Safety Guidelines	139
Local Transportation Regulations	142
Social norms	145
Emergency Contacts	148
Travel Tips for a Smooth Stay	**151**
Language Basics	151
Currency and Payment	153
WiFi and Connectivity	155
Tip for Solo Travelers	158
Last Thoughts and Resources	161
Conclusion	**164**

Introductions

As I got off the train at São Bento station in Porto, the air was laced with nostalgia and excitement. The station's grandeur, with elaborate azulejo tiles representing events from Portuguese history, set the tone for my journey around this fascinating city. Porto, with its rich culture and breathtaking scenery, offered an experience unlike any other.

My first trip was in the famed Ribeira neighborhood. The colorful structures along the Douro River seemed to be painted by a child's imagination. I walked along the small cobblestone lanes, where laughing and the aroma of grilled sardines filled the air. It was a Saturday, and the riverfront was alive with activity. Street musicians strummed their guitars, while merchants peddled everything from handcrafted items to tasty pastries.

Feeling daring, I decided to try a "francesinha," a local sandwich known for its heartiness. I discovered a little, family-owned eatery situated away from the tourist circuit. As I took my first mouthful, I was hit with layers of flavor: delicious sausage, tender beef, and a spicy sauce that left me wanting more. Each taste was a tribute to Porto's culinary heritage, and I relished every bite.

After my dinner, I visited the Dom Luís I Bridge. The view from the top was spectacular; the river glimmered in the sun, and the city's terracotta roofs spread out in front of me. As I stood there, I felt a tremendous connection to Porto's past. The bridge, built in 1886, was a triumph of engineering that has lasted the test of time. I took images to capture the scene, but nothing could properly convey the sense of being there, overlooking such beauty.

I crossed the bridge and went to Vila Nova de Gaia, which is noted for its wine cellars. Porto is famed for its port wine, so I was keen to discover more. I picked a cellar that provided tours and tastings. As I arrived, the chilly, darkly lighted area welcomed me with the perfume of aging barrels. The guide described the winemaking process, stressing the significance of the region's terroir. I discovered that the Douro Valley, where the grapes are cultivated, has a peculiar microclimate that adds to the wine's characteristic taste.

The tour's highlight was the tasting session. I tried a variety of ports, from the rich, sweet Ruby to the complicated Tawny. With each taste, I admired the artistry that went into each bottle. As I sipped a glass of Vintage port, I felt grateful for the experiences Porto had previously provided me.

As darkness arrived, I returned to the Ribeira neighborhood. The sun started to set, giving a golden tint over the river. I discovered a little patio where I could have a glass of Vinho Verde, a light, refreshing wine unique to the area. I leaned back and listened to the sounds of the city waking up as the nightlife started to pulse. Locals gathered for supper, laughing rang out from surrounding cafés, and a beautiful glow of lights reflected off the lake.

In the middle of this environment, I started up a discussion with the couple sitting next to me. They were from Lisbon and revealed their favorite places in the city, encouraging me to go outside the typical tourist routes. Their excitement was contagious, so I decided to join them for dinner at a local seafood restaurant. We ordered a feast of fresh seafood, along with local greens and, of course, more wine.

Throughout the lunch, we exchanged tales and laughed, bonding over our passion for travel and adventure. They informed me about the lively Fado music culture in Porto, a genre rich in passion and history. Intrigued, I made preparations to attend a Fado performance later that evening.

After supper, I walked the old alleys of Miragaia, where I discovered a little pub having a Fado night. The vibe changed as I arrived. The dark lighting, wooden furniture, and aroma of traditional Portuguese cuisine created an intimate atmosphere. I sank, and the first sounds of Fado filled the air. The vocalist, a lady in a flowing black garment, poured her heart into each line, creating stories of desire and love. The music wrapped around me like a loving hug, taking me to the heart of Portuguese culture.

As the night progressed, I reminisced about my day in Porto. I sampled the cuisine, relished the wine, and learned about the history and music that marked this amazing city. Each event was a thread in the rich fabric of Porto, connecting the past and present, local and global.

The next morning, I awoke to the light flowing through my window, anxious to explore more. I chose to go to Livraria Lello, one of the most gorgeous bookshops in the world. As I entered, I was drawn to the staircase, a whirling piece of beauty. I gazed at the book-lined shelves, the woodwork carvings, and the stained-glass skylight above. It was a literary refuge, and I lost myself among the books, deciding which tales to take home with me.

My final trip was to the Palácio da Bolsa, a neoclassical structure that originally housed the stock market. The opulent interiors were a visual feast, and the Arab Room's unique patterns left me speechless. I learned about Porto's commercial history and how it created the city we know today.

As I prepared to leave Porto, I experienced a range of emotions. This city has provided me with a treasure mine of memories, including wonderful cuisine, a rich history, and the friendliness of its people. As I boarded the train, I knew I'd always have a piece of Porto with me, its beauty and energy staying in my heart long after I'd gone home.

History and Significance.

Porto, Portugal's second-largest city, combines tradition and contemporary flawlessly. Porto, located along the Douro River, has a lengthy history dating back to ancient times when it was known as Portus Cale, a name that later evolved into Portugal.

The city's history dates back to the Roman period when it was a thriving harbor. Porto has had several rulers throughout the years, from the Visigoths to the Moors, all of whom have left their stamp on the city's rich tapestry. In 868, Alfonso III of Asturias regained Porto from the Moors, paving the way for the city's crucial role in Portugal's national development.

Porto's importance expanded during the Middle Ages, notably in the 14th and 15th centuries, when it became a major commercial and shipbuilding center. In 1394, Prince Henry the Navigator was born, becoming an important character in the Age of Discoveries. His excursions from Porto's shipyards established new commercial channels and boosted Portugal's global power.

The city's fortitude was tested during the Napoleonic Wars, when British troops headed by Arthur Wellesley, later Duke of Wellington, crossed the Douro River and rescued Porto from French rule in 1809. This win demonstrates Porto's strategic significance and the resilient character of its people.

Porto's architectural legacy is very stunning. The city's cathedral, initially a 12th-century Romanesque construction, now has Gothic cloisters and Baroque embellishments that illustrate the city's changing architectural styles. The Church of São Martinho de Cedofeita, with beautifully carved capitals, serves as a reminder of Porto's early Christian heritage.

The growing port wine business propelled Porto into a golden period in the 18th century. The city's shipyards and warehouses along the Douro River became linked with this world-famous wine, which remains a significant export and source of local pride.

Today, Porto's old center, a UNESCO World Heritage site since 1996, welcomes tourists to explore its small alleyways, which are dotted with colorful houses and characteristic azulejos. The Dom Luís I Bridge, an iconic landmark of Porto, provides breathtaking views of the city and river below.

When to Visit.

Porto, with its picturesque streets and rich culture, welcomes travelers all year round. However, the greatest time to come is determined by what you want to experience.

From June to September, Porto has pleasant, sunny weather, making it ideal for outdoor activities and events. In June, the city hosts events such as Serralves em Festa, a non-stop arts festival lasting 50 hours, and Festa de São João, which features music, dancing, and fireworks in the streets. During these months, temperatures remain around a moderate 23°C (73°F), with rare heatwaves pushing the mercury higher. This is also the peak tourist season, so anticipate crowded streets and increased hotel rates. However, the vibrant atmosphere and lengthy days make the stay worthwhile.

Springtime, from March to May, is another excellent season to visit Porto. The climate is pleasant, with temperatures ranging from 15°C to 20°C (59°F to 68°F), and the city's parks and gardens are in full bloom. This season is ideal for taking strolls along the Douro River and seeing the old Ribeira region without the summer throng. Easter events give a distinct cultural flavor, particularly in neighboring Braga, which is famous for its huge processions.

Autumn, from October to November, provides a calmer, more relaxed atmosphere. The weather continues nice, with temperatures comparable to spring, and the summer throngs have dwindled. The Douro Valley wineries are now harvesting grapes, making this an ideal time for wine connoisseurs. You may enjoy wine tastings and lovely drives across the countryside while taking in the fall colors.

Winter, from December to February, is Porto's off-season. The weather is colder, with average temperatures ranging from 10°C to 15°C (50°F to 59°F), and there is a greater risk of rain. However, this is the perfect moment to explore Porto as a native. The city's charming cafés and restaurants provide a welcoming sanctuary, and you may visit cultural attractions without crowds. Winter adds its appeal with spectacular Christmas markets and decorations.

No matter when you arrive, Porto's rich history, breathtaking architecture, and lively culture guarantee that there is always something to see and do. Whether you're drinking port wine by the river in the summer or visiting the city's museums in the winter, Porto will provide an amazing experience.

Getting to Porto.

Getting to this dynamic metropolis is easy owing to its well-connected transportation options. If you're flying in, Francisco Sá Carneiro Airport is your first stop. This modern airport, located around 11 kilometers from the city center, handles a large number of international and local flights. From the airport, take the metro to the city center, which takes about 25 minutes. Taxis and ride-sharing services are also easily accessible, providing a more direct path to your lodging.

São Bento Railway Station is a must-see for rail passengers. This ancient station, embellished with exquisite azulejo tiles, is strategically positioned and serves important cities in Portugal and beyond. High-speed trains from Lisbon arrive in less than three hours, making it a practical alternative for visitors visiting the country.

Buses are another inexpensive option to get to the city. Several firms run routes from major European cities, with luxurious coaches dropping you off at the main bus station, which is a short walk from the city center. If you're traveling from Spain, the trip is picturesque and very short, particularly from adjacent places like Vigo.

Driving allows you to explore at your speed. The city is well-connected by roads, and the travel from Lisbon takes around three hours. However, navigating the tight, twisting streets may be difficult, so it's generally advisable to park and use public transportation to go about.

For a more leisurely approach, try coming by cruise ship. The Leixões Cruise Terminal in Matosinhos is conveniently positioned close to the city. From here, take a shuttle or cab to your destination, taking in the coastline vistas along the way.

One Week Itinerary

A week in this enchanting city provides an ideal balance of history, culture, and leisure. Begin your tour in the historic center, where you may explore the small lanes of the Ribeira area. This region, with its vibrant architecture and dynamic atmosphere, is a UNESCO World Heritage site. On your first day, visit the São Bento Railway Station, known for its beautiful azulejo tiles, and the Sé Cathedral, which provides panoramic views of the city.

On your second day, take the Dom Luís I Bridge to Vila Nova de Gaia. You may tour the famous port wine cellars and taste this world-renowned wine. Take a leisurely walk along the waterfront, or consider a river cruise to experience the city from a fresh perspective.

Day three is ideal for exploring the local culture. Visit the Bolhão Market to experience fresh products and local delights. After that, visit Livraria Lello, one of the world's most beautiful bookshops, and then unwind in the tranquil Jardins do Palácio de Cristal, which has breathtaking views of the Douro River.

Midweek, take a day excursion to the Douro Valley, a UNESCO World Heritage site noted for its terraced vineyards and magnificent scenery. Take a wine tour and taste at one of the numerous quintas, and consider taking a lovely boat trip down the Douro River.

On Day 5, experience the city's creative side. Visit the Serralves Museum of Contemporary Art, which is nestled in lovely grounds, followed by the Soares dos Reis National Museum, which has a collection of Portuguese art. In the evening, attend a performance at the Casa da Música, a contemporary music venue.

On Day 6, visit Guimarães, often known as Portugal's birthplace. Explore the ancient castle and the Dukes of Braganza Palace, as well as the lovely historic city.

Finish your week with a quiet day at the beach. Go to Matosinhos, a short metro trip away, to enjoy the sandy beaches and tasty seafood. In the evening, return to the city for a farewell supper at one of the many outstanding restaurants, eating traditional foods and reminiscing on your memorable week.

Practical Information

As you plan your vacation, here are some vital recommendations to ensure a seamless and pleasurable experience.

First and foremost, getting about is easy. The city's public transportation system is both efficient and inexpensive. You may tour other neighborhoods by using the metro, bus, or tram. Grab an Andante Card, which can be loaded with credit and used across several means of transportation. If you arrive by automobile, park on the outskirts and use public transportation to traverse the city center's tight, congested streets.

Booking ahead of time is essential for lodging, particularly if you wish to stay in popular places such as Ribeira or Aliados. These districts combine ancient elegance with contemporary facilities, but they may rapidly fill up, especially during busy tourist seasons. Consider lodging at Foz do Douro for a more relaxing environment while being just a short tram ride from the city center.

This city's dining scene is a culinary delight. From traditional Portuguese delicacies to Michelin-starred eateries, there's something for everyone's taste. Try local favorites such as "francesinha" and fresh fish. To prevent excessive wait times, make reservations, particularly at popular sites. Don't forget to accompany your meal with a drink of the region's famed Port wine.

For those who like shopping, the city provides a range of possibilities. Unique souvenirs and presents may be found at high-end stores as well as lovely rural marketplaces. The Bolhão Market is a must-see for fresh products and local cuisine. If you're searching for something more modern, go to Rua de Santa Catarina, a lively retail strip featuring a mix of foreign and local stores.

Weatherwise, the city has a moderate climate, although it's always a good idea to be prepared. Summer might be hot, so bring light clothes and sunscreen. Winters are pleasant but may be wet, so a waterproof jacket and comfy shoes are required. Because of the city's steep geography, you'll be walking a lot, so bring some comfortable shoes.

Finally, here are some cultural pointers to bear in mind. While English is commonly spoken, knowing a few basic Portuguese words will greatly enhance your trip. The villagers are nice and appreciate your efforts. Also, tipping is not required but is appreciated, particularly in restaurants and for excellent service.

Navigating the City

Transport Options

This attractive city's transit choices are well-connected and diversified, making it easy to get about. Whether you're touring the historic core or heading to the gorgeous surroundings, there's a form of transportation to fit any traveler's requirements.

The metro system is popular among both inhabitants and tourists. With its clean, fast, and regular services, it links major regions, including the airport. The metro lines are color-coded, making navigating easy even for first-time tourists. The Andante card is your greatest friend here, providing a simple and inexpensive method to pay for journeys on the metro, buses, and even certain trains.

Buses have a large network and may reach portions of the city that the metro cannot. The blue and white buses are simple to see, and although the routes may appear confusing at first, the STCP app is a useful tool for planning your trip. For a more picturesque ride, take one of the vintage trams. These lovely cars rattle along the tiny streets, providing a nostalgic peek into the past while transporting you to some of the city's most scenic locations.

Taxis and ride-sharing services such as Uber are easily accessible for those moments when you want fast and direct transport. They are especially beneficial late at night or when you are carrying heavy shopping bags. The funicular and the Gaia cable car provide a unique vista. The funicular provides a short but steep trip with spectacular views of the river, and the cable car glides over the Port wine cellars, affording a panoramic overview of the metropolis.

If you arrive by airline, the metro is the most convenient method to go from the airport to the city center. Alternatively, shuttle services and taxis are available to take you away. For those who prefer the freedom of driving, automobile rentals are available, albeit parking may be difficult in busy places.

Walking is another excellent method to explore. The city center is full of sights, including the renowned Dom Luís I Bridge and the vibrant Ribeira area. Many of the streets are pedestrian-friendly, letting you enjoy the scene at your speed.

São Bento and Campanhã stations provide good rail services for day vacations. They link you to surrounding beauties like the Douro Valley, famed for its wine, and the seaside town of Aveiro, often known as the "Venice of Portugal."

In essence, exploring this dynamic city is both simple and entertaining, with a number of transportation alternatives available to suit every style and plan. Whether you're flying through the streets on a tram, sailing along the river, or just wandering through the old lanes, each route adds another dimension of discovery to your vacation.

Public Transportation Guide

Navigating this dynamic city is a pleasure, owing to its rapid and diverse public transportation system. The metro is a prominent feature, with sleek trains and well-kept stops. It's a fast and dependable means to move about, linking major locations and even reaching the airport. The Andante card is a must-have for seamless travel throughout the metro, buses, and certain trains.

Buses are another fantastic choice since they cover a large network and reach regions that the metro does not. The blue and white buses are simple to see, and although the routes may appear complicated at first, the STCP app is a lifesaver for arranging your journeys. The vintage trams provide a nostalgic way to experience the city. These ancient automobiles crash along the small streets, providing an unusual viewpoint of the city's charm.

Taxis and ride-sharing services like Uber are numerous and handy, particularly for late-night trips or while carrying large luggage. For a picturesque journey, the funicular and Gaia cable car are excellent options. The funicular provides a short but steep ride with beautiful views of the river, whilst the cable car glides over the Port wine cellars, affording a stunning perspective of the city.

Arriving by plane? The metro is the most direct route from the airport to the city center, however, shuttle services and taxis are also available. If you prefer to drive, automobile rentals are available; however, parking might be difficult in congested places.

Walking is an excellent method to explore, particularly in the tight city center. The streets are pedestrian-friendly, so you can take in the sights at your speed. From the majestic Dom Luís I Bridge to the vibrant Ribeira area, there is enough to explore on foot.

São Bento and Campanhã stations provide good rail services for day vacations. They link you to local sites like the Douro Valley, which is noted for its wine, and the seaside town of Aveiro, also known as the "Venice of Portugal."

Walking Tours.

Begin your tour in the historic Ribeira neighborhood, where colorful houses flank the Douro River. This UNESCO World Heritage site is alive with activity, from riverbank cafés to street entertainers. As you explore through the small lanes, you'll come across hidden jewels like traditional stores and local cafés that serve exquisite pastéis de nata.

Explore the Dom Luís I Bridge for breathtaking views of the city and river. After crossing the bridge, you'll arrive at Vila Nova de Gaia, which is famed for its port wine cellars. Join a guided tour to learn about the history of port wine and have a sampling.

Return over the river and up the steep streets to the Sé Cathedral. This Romanesque edifice, with its stunning façade and panoramic vistas, is a must-see. The nearby São Bento Railway Station is a must-see for its stunning azulejo tiles representing historical events in Portugal.

Wander the Bolhão Market, a vibrant local center. Vendors provide fresh vegetables, seafood, and traditional cuisines. It's a terrific spot to experience local culture and perhaps pick up some mementos.

For a cultural experience, visit the Livraria Lello, one of the world's most magnificent bookshops. Its breathtaking design, complete with a grand staircase and stained glass ceiling, is supposed to have inspired J.K. Rowling was write Harry Potter.

Complete your walking trip at the Boavista area, where you may unwind in the tranquil Crystal Palace Gardens. The rich foliage and peaceful ambiance provide an ideal retreat from the city's rush and bustle.

Whether you're a history buff, a gourmet, or just seeking a nice stroll, this city has something for everyone. Each step exposes a new tale, sight, and experience, resulting in a unique destination.

Biking in Porto.

Exploring this city on two wheels is an experience that mixes the pleasure of riding with the allure of uncovering hidden gems and gorgeous roads. The city's varied topography and gorgeous sights make it an excellent destination for cyclists of all skill levels.

Begin your ride along the Douro River, where the flat riverfront trails provide a relaxing start. The lovely air and sight of classic Rabelo boats drifting past established a peaceful atmosphere. Pedal past the beautiful Ribeira area and towards the Dom Luís I Bridge. Crossing this landmark bridge on the bike is an unforgettable experience, with panoramic views of the city and river below.

After crossing the bridge, go into Vila Nova de Gaia. This region is famed for its port wine cellars, and several of them provide bike excursions. It's an excellent chance to learn about local winemaking traditions while taking a soothing respite.

For those wanting a little more of a challenge, the trek up to the Crystal Palace Gardens is certainly worth it. The beautiful gardens and breathtaking views of the city make this an ideal area to relax and enjoy the atmosphere. The fall from here is thrilling, with twisting lanes taking you back to the city center.

Another must-ride route is the beach trail to Foz do Douro. This journey takes you along the Atlantic coast, where you can enjoy the salty sea air and the sound of waves breaking on the beach. The trail is studded with cafés and beach bars, which are ideal for a brief refueling break.

Experience local life by cycling around the Bolhão Market neighborhood. The busy market lanes are lined with merchants offering fresh vegetables, fish, and traditional foods. It's a busy place to explore the city's colorful culture and perhaps pick up some local goodies.

End your riding excursion in the Boavista neighborhood, where broad avenues and contemporary buildings provide a unique view of the city. The neighboring Serralves Park, with its lovely gardens and modern art museum, is a relaxing spot to end your journey.

Safety Tips

Walking through the colorful streets of this Portuguese jewel, it's easy to get engrossed in its charm and beauty. However, keeping a few safety considerations in mind might help ensure that your visit goes as well as possible.

The city is relatively secure, but like with any famous tourist attraction, it is prudent to exercise caution. Petty theft, including pickpocketing, may occur in busy settings including public transit, markets, and tourist hotspots[1]. Keep your possessions safe, and avoid flashing costly goods.

When touring the historic areas, be aware of your surroundings. The small, twisting lanes are beautiful yet may be perplexing. It's a good idea to have a map or a dependable navigation app nearby. If you're lost, don't be afraid to ask locals for directions; they're typically pleasant and happy to assist.

At night, stick to well-lit and crowded locations. The city offers a vibrant nightlife, but avoid poorly lit streets and alleyways. If you're out late, consider utilizing trusted taxi services or ridesharing applications to securely return to your lodging.

Be careful with your valuables. Use money belts or concealed pockets to protect your passport, cash, and credit cards. When eating out, keep an eye on your luggage and avoid leaving them hanging on the back of your chair.

If you want to hire a car, be aware that theft from automobiles is possible. Avoid leaving valuables visible, and park in safe, well-lit places. Alternatively, the city's public transit system is efficient and may provide a safer way to travel about.

Street scams may be prevalent in tourist-heavy locations. Be aware of excessively pleasant people who offer unsolicited aid or attempt to sell you anything. It is usually better to respectfully refuse and move on.

Those who like a drink or two should be aware of their alcohol usage. It's tempting to get carried away with the local wine, but remaining alert to your surroundings is critical. Drink responsibly and keep an eye on your beverage at all times.

Finally, keep up with local news and any possible safety problems. Your lodging hosts might be an excellent source for up-to-date information on regions to avoid current difficulties.

Must-see Attractions

Ribeira District.

Ribeira is a lovely area that embodies the spirit of its city via its dynamic atmosphere and gorgeous environment. This medieval district on the Douro River is a UNESCO World Heritage Site, famed for its colorful homes, narrow cobblestone alleyways, and bustling waterfront.

As you go through Ribeira, you'll be met with classic Portuguese buildings covered with azulejos (ceramic tiles) in a variety of colors. These buildings, placed tightly together, provide a distinct and visually attractive environment ideal for a stroll. The district's main plaza, Praça da Ribeira, is a busy center where both residents and visitors congregate to enjoy the vibrant atmosphere. Here, you'll discover a range of cafés and restaurants serving wonderful Portuguese food, as well as outdoor seating that's ideal for people-watching.

Ribeira's Dom Luís I Bridge, created by Gustave Eiffel's pupil, is a must-see attraction. This double-deck iron bridge links the neighborhood to Vila Nova de Gaia and provides spectacular views of the river and town. Walking over the bridge is a must-do activity, particularly around sunset.

Ribeira is also home to several famous landmarks. The Palácio da Bolsa, also known as the Stock Exchange Palace, is a majestic palace with a lavishly designed interior that represents the city's richness and history. The Igreja de São

Francisco, with its Gothic construction and exquisite Baroque interior, is one of the area's most stunning churches.

For those interested in history, the Casa do Infante, or House of the Prince, is a must-see. This ancient edifice, dating back to the 14th century, today contains a museum that provides insight into the city's history and maritime legacy.

As night strikes, The district's pubs and clubs are alive with music and laughter, providing a diverse range of entertainment alternatives. Ribeira offers something for everyone, whether you want to relax by the river or party all night.

In addition to its cultural and historical features, Ribeira is an excellent spot to explore the local way of life. The district's markets and stores sell a variety of things, from fresh vegetables to handcrafted crafts, and provide a look into the life of its citizens.

Livraria Lello.

Livraria Lello is a book lover's dream and an architectural masterpiece that attracts people from all over the globe. This historic bookshop, often regarded as one of the most beautiful in the world, is a must-see for anybody visiting the city.

Stepping inside, you're impressed by the gorgeous neo-Gothic decor. The beautiful woodwork carvings, stained glass skylight, and grand staircase combine to create an almost mystical environment. It's no surprise that this location is said to have inspired J.K. Rowling was writing the Harry Potter series.

The shelves are stacked with volumes of every type, from classic classics to recent blockbusters. Whether you are a bibliophile or just searching for a one-of-a-kind keepsake, there is something for everyone. The staff is educated and enthusiastic about books, and they are always eager to help you discover your next great read.

One of the features of Livraria Lello is its second story, where you can take in the view of the whole shop from above. The balcony provides an excellent vantage point to admire the architectural elements and lively activities below. It's an excellent location for taking photos or just enjoying the atmosphere.

In addition to its extensive book collection, Livraria Lello conducts a variety of cultural events, such as book signings, readings, and exhibits. These events contribute to the thriving cultural environment and provide opportunities to interact with local and international writers.

Another appealing aspect of the bookshop is its café. You may have a cup of coffee or a bottle of wine while exploring your most recent purchase. The café's pleasant environment makes it an ideal location to unwind after a day of touring.

Dom Luís I Bridge

The Dom Luís I Bridge crosses the Douro River and connects the city to Vila Nova de Gaia. It is a remarkable double-deck metal arch bridge. This bridge, designed by the gifted Théophile Seyrig, a pupil of the legendary Gustave Eiffel, is an engineering wonder and tribute to late-nineteenth-century inventiveness.

Walking over the bridge is an event in and of itself. The top deck, which is shared with the metro, provides stunning views of the river and its surroundings. From this vantage point, you can view the terracotta roofs, twisting streets, and lively activity underneath. The lower deck, on the other hand, is accessible to people and cars, allowing for a closer look at the beautiful ironwork and busy activity along the riverside.

The bridge was opened in 1886 and has since become an iconic emblem. Its construction was in response to the rising demand for a more solid link between the two sides of the river, and it replaced the ancient suspension bridge that had previously been there. The design competition for the bridge included submissions from numerous notable engineers of the period, but Seyrig's concept eventually won out.

As you go over the top deck, you'll note the bridge's remarkable span, which was the longest of its type when it was constructed. The views from here are breathtaking, particularly after sunset, when the city is bathed in a golden light. The lower deck, although less high, has its appeal, providing a closer perspective of river traffic and everyday activity along the quays.

On the Gaia side, there's a busy district with wine cellars, cafés, and stores. This is the ideal area to relax and have a drink of the renowned local wine while admiring the views of the bridge and metropolis. The region is also recognized for its bright street art and cultural events, making it an ideal location for discovering and experiencing local culture.

The Dom Luís I Bridge caters to a variety of interests, including history, architecture, and scenic walks. Its combination of historical importance, architectural beauty, and breathtaking vistas makes it a must-see attraction. So take your time, enjoy the trek, and let the bridge's elegance enchant you.

Porto Cathedral

The Porto Cathedral, known locally as Sé do Porto, is a remarkable example of the city's rich history and architectural progress. This Romanesque-Gothic edifice, positioned on a hilltop, has a commanding view of the surrounding region, making it a visible landmark.

As you approach the cathedral, the first thing you notice is its majestic façade, flanked by two sturdy towers. The façade, with its crenelated walls and tiny windows, emanates a fortress-like air, indicating its 12th-century origins. Stepping inside, you're met with a calm, even austere interior that contrasts strongly with the extravagant Baroque embellishments added in the following years.

One of the highlights is the exquisite rose window, a superb example of Gothic artistry that casts a delicate, ethereal light over the nave. The cloisters, which were built in the 14th century, are another must-see. Their Gothic arches and beautiful azulejo tilework portraying religious motifs provide a tranquil respite from the hectic metropolis outside.

The cathedral's treasury has an impressive collection of holy art, including gilded altarpieces, delicate jewelry, and religious garments. Each artwork offers a tale of dedication and craftsmanship, highlighting the cathedral's role as a spiritual and cultural center.

Don't pass up the opportunity to ascend the tiny stairway to the summit of the tower. The panoramic views from here are just spectacular, providing a unique viewpoint of the city's red-tiled roofs and the flowing Douro River underneath.

The Episcopal Palace, located next to the church, is another architectural wonder worth seeing. Its towering Baroque façade and rich interiors provide an intriguing peek into the life of the city's bishops over the years.

Whether you're an architectural fan, a history buff, or just searching for a quiet place to ponder, the Porto Cathedral provides a rich tapestry of experiences. Its unique combination of Romanesque, Gothic, and Baroque characteristics, together with its historical importance, make it a must-see trip. Take your time exploring every nook and corner, and let the cathedral's ageless beauty and quiet atmosphere enchant you.

Wine Cellars in Vila Nova de Gaia.

Vila Nova de Gaia, located just over the Douro River, is a wine lover's paradise. This lovely neighborhood is home to some of the most prestigious wine cellars, where the enchantment of port wine is brought to life. As you walk down the riverbank, the air is thick with the rich perfume of aged wine, beckoning you to visit the cellars that have been practicing their skill for generations.

One of the attractions is Taylor's, a historic cellar that provides not only a taste of their superb ports but also a tour through their history. The tour is immersive, with interpreters presenting intriguing insights about the wine-making process and the family's past. Following the tour, the tasting area offers a tranquil atmosphere to sip their best choices while admiring magnificent views of the Douro River.

Graham's, another well-known port wine producer, is only a short walk away. Graham's cellar tour offers an in-depth look at the art of wine aging, complete with rows upon rows of oak barrels and vats. The tasting experience here is superb, with a diverse selection of ports that demonstrate the depth and complexity of their products. The patio at Graham's is an ideal place to unwind with a glass of their 20-year-old Tawny while admiring the gorgeous environment.

For a more modern experience, go to Sandeman. Sandeman is known for its unusual caped man logo, which mixes heritage and contemporary. The guided tour is interactive, with multimedia displays that bring the history of port wine to life. The tasting session includes a selection of their greatest ports, combined with local specialties that complement the tastes.

If you want a more intimate atmosphere, Calem is an excellent alternative. This family-owned cellar provides a warm environment and individual tours. The guides are enthusiastic and informed, so the trip is both informative and pleasant. Calem's tasting area is pleasant, with a range of ports suitable for both beginners and specialists.

A visit to Vila Nova de Gaia is incomplete without a trip to the World of Wine (WOW) complex. This cultural neighborhood is all about wine, with several museums, restaurants, and stores. The Wine Experience Museum is especially interesting, with interactive displays that illustrate the complexities of wine production and tasting. It's an excellent location to expand your appreciation for wine in a pleasant and interesting setting.

As you explore through the tiny alleyways and along the riverbank, you'll come across countless smaller cellars and wine bars, each with its distinct charm. These hidden jewels can provide more customized encounters as well as the opportunity to learn about lesser-known port wine kinds.

São Bento Train Station

Explore the historic São Bento Railway Station, where time appears to stand still. This architectural marvel, which opened in 1916, is more than simply a transportation hub; it's a representation of Portugal's rich history. As you go through its majestic entryway, you're welcomed with beautiful azulejo tiles on the walls. Jorge Colaço's beautifully painted blue and white tiles show themes from Portugal's past, including royal conquests and country life. It's like walking into a living museum, with each tile telling a tale.

The station was constructed by famous architect José Marques da Silva, who combined French Beaux-Arts elements with indigenous influences. The facade, with its traditional stone façade, alludes to the grandeur inside. The inside, however, is genuinely captivating. The main hall is 551 square meters in size and has approximately 20,000 tiles. These tiles were put between 1905 and 1916 and are now considered one of the best examples of azulejo art in the nation.

Aside from its artistic charm, the station is a thriving hive of activity. Trains link numerous regions of the region, making them an important component of many inhabitants' everyday lives. Whether you're taking a train to the Douro Valley or just passing through, the station's attractiveness is apparent. The steady flow of visitors adds to the lively atmosphere, making it an ideal location for people-watching.

The station's location is great for seeing the surrounding sights. A short walk away is the Church of Santo António dos Congregados, which has a stunning azulejo façade. The old Ribeira quarter, with its tiny streets and riverfront vistas, is also easily accessible. Don't miss the opportunity to walk over the renowned Dom Luís I Bridge, which provides breathtaking views of the city and Douro River.

São Bento Railway Station is more than just a rail station; it's a historical and artistic experience. This station is a must-see for anybody who enjoys history, and art, or just wants to immerse themselves in local culture. So take your time, appreciate the nuances, and let the tales of the past unfold around you.

Palácio de Bolsa

Step inside the grandeur of Palácio da Bolsa, a 19th-century masterpiece that reflects the city's rich trade heritage. This architectural masterpiece, situated in the center of the historical area, was built by the Commercial Association to represent the wealth and power of local merchants.

As you approach, the Neoclassical façade, with its massive columns and beautiful brickwork, draws your eye. The building's appearance alluded to the wealth inside, but nothing prepared you for the majesty that greets you inside.

The Pátio das Nações, often known as the Nations' Courtyard, welcomes visitors upon entry. This central atrium is surmounted by a beautiful octagonal dome made of iron and glass, which provides natural light to the room. The lower half of the dome is ornamented with coats of arms from nations that had trading links with Portugal in the nineteenth century, an homage to the structure's economic origins.

The Arab Room will surely be a highlight of your stay. This chamber, inspired by Granada's Alhambra, is a Moorish Revival masterpiece. Its walls are decorated with elaborate stucco work, gilded sculptures, and brilliant tiles, resulting in a stunning display of color and skill. The room's magnificence made it ideal for entertaining dignitaries and kings, and it continues to captivate tourists today.

As you go through the hallways, you'll see the great staircase created by Gonçalves e Sousa. This marble masterpiece is studded with sculptures and busts of famous personalities, rising to the higher levels where more treasures await. The Tribunal Room, with its rich wood paneling and intricate ornamentation, provides a look into the court processes that were formerly held here.

The Palácio da Bolsa is more than simply a visual feast; it also functions as a living museum. Guided tours provide intriguing details about the building's history, design, and the critical role it played in the city's economic life. This castle provides a compelling voyage through time for architectural enthusiasts, history buffs, and inquisitive travelers alike.

Don't pass up the opportunity to explore this renowned monument, where every corner tells a fresh narrative and every feature evokes a bygone period of grandeur and grace.

Market of Bolhão.

Since 1837, Mercado do Bolhão has been the city's central market. This historic jewel, located in a magnificently restored Beaux-Arts structure, is a must-see for anybody wishing to enjoy local culture and cuisine.

As you go into the market, you'll be welcomed by a busy environment filled with the sounds of merchants shouting out their products and the rich fragrances of fresh fruit, seafood, and meat. The market is divided into three levels, each of which provides a distinct perspective on city life. The bottom level has a variety of vendors offering anything from fresh fruits and vegetables to fragrant herbs and spices. The fishmongers showcase their catch of the day, which includes dazzling fish and shellfish that seem to have just been taken from the water.

Moving up to the second level, butchers display a range of meats, including luscious cuts of beef and typical Portuguese sausages. The market also has numerous family-run enterprises that have been handed down through generations, providing a more personalized shopping experience. Don't pass up the opportunity to try some local cheeses and cured meats, which are ideal for a picnic or a light lunch.

The upper level has a mix of modern additions, including fashionable coffee shops and small eateries. These areas are ideal for taking a break and enjoying a cup of coffee or a quick lunch while taking in the market's lively ambiance. Some of the restaurants provide traditional Portuguese foods, providing a taste of local cuisine without leaving the market.

Mercado do Bolhão has unique items in addition to its culinary offerings. Everyone may find something for themselves, from handcrafted jewelry to locally manufactured fragrances. You may also discover merchants that provide services such as knife sharpening, which adds to the market's appeal and functionality.

The market's recent renovation has kept its traditional elegance while also modernizing its amenities, making it more accessible and entertaining for tourists. The structure itself is impressive, with its magnificent grandeur and numerous embellishments that represent its long history.

Mercado do Bolhão is a must-visit for foodies, shoppers searching for unusual items, and those who appreciate visiting lively marketplaces. It's a location where tradition and modernity coexist, and each visit seems like a fresh experience.

Casa de Música

Casa da Música exemplifies contemporary architecture and cultural energy. The famous architect Rem Koolhaas designed this music hall, which opened in 2005 and has since become a landmark. Its distinctive, angular shape is awe-inspiring, attracting tourists from all over the world to admire its unique construction.

The building itself is a piece of art, with its strong lines and creative use of space. The acoustics inside are world-class, making it an ideal setting for a variety of musical acts. From classical symphonies to current jazz, the programming is both wide and outstanding. The main music hall, with its cutting-edge sound equipment, provides an unforgettable aural experience.

Casa do Música serves as a cultural exchange and education center in addition to its musical offerings. It organizes seminars, talks, and exhibits to build a thriving community of artists and aficionados. The facility also has numerous smaller performance areas, each intended to highlight the style of music being presented.

Visitors may join guided tours to learn more about the architectural and acoustic elements that make this facility unique. Tours often include behind-the-scenes glances at rehearsal rooms and technical facilities, giving visitors a better understanding of the artistry and engineering involved.

The site is convenient, being on Avenida da Boavista, one of the major thoroughfares. This makes it easier for residents and visitors to attend events. The surrounding neighborhood is bustling, with several cafés and restaurants where you may get a meal or a drink before or after the show..

Jardim do Morro.

Jardim do Morro, located on the southern bank of the Douro River, is a lush oasis that provides a peaceful retreat from the metropolitan bustle. This lovely garden in Vila Nova de Gaia is popular with both residents and tourists, offering a fantastic place to relax and take in the spectacular views of the old metropolis across the river.

The garden's name, which means "Garden on the Hill," is particularly appropriate. As you walk over its well-kept walkways, you'll be surrounded by lush grass and colorful flower beds. The aroma of blossoming flowers fills the air, and the soft rustling of leaves serves as a pleasant soundtrack to your promenade.

The panoramic views are one of the green haven's features. From numerous vantage points across the garden, you can observe the Douro River snake its way through the city. The Dom Luís I Bridge, with its double-deck construction, connects the two sides of the river. Since its construction in 1886, this engineering wonder has served as a regional emblem.

As the day comes to a close, Jardim do Morro changes into a wonderful setting for watching the sunset. The sky is painted in orange and pink, and the reflections on the river make a stunning image. It's a favorite hangout for photographers and romantics looking to capture the essence of the event.

The garden also has historical value. It was previously part of the grounds of the Serra do Pilar Monastery, an Augustinian monastery established in 1670. Because of its strategic position on both sides of the river, this monastery played an important role during the city's siege in the nineteenth century. Today, the monastery is a UNESCO World Heritage site with a military museum, providing a historical backdrop to your visit.

Jardim do Morro presents a variety of cultural events and festivals year-round. One of the most prominent is the São João Festival, which is held every June. The area becomes a bustling center of activity, with fireworks lighting up the sky and celebrations spilling out into the neighboring streets.

Getting to Jardim do Morro is simple. Take Metro Line D to Jardim do Morro station or walk over the Dom Luís I Bridge from the other side of the river. The ride itself provides breathtaking vistas, making it an ideal precursor to your stay.

Whether you want to relax with a picnic beneath a tree, learn about the area's history, or just enjoy the breathtaking views, Jardim do Morro is a must-see site. It's a location where nature, history, and culture come together to provide a one-of-a-kind and unforgettable experience.

Culinary Delights.

Traditional Dishes To Try

Wandering through the lovely alleyways of this northern Portuguese jewel will satisfy your taste sensations. The local cuisine is a delectable combination of robust tastes and soothing meals that represent the region's rich culinary history. Here are several must-try classic foods, along with where to locate them and how much you can expect to spend.

Begin with Francesinha, a renowned sandwich that serves as a whole meal. This decadent dish is stacked with ham, sausage, and steak, all topped with melted cheese and drowned in a spicy beer and tomato sauce. It's a full and tasty meal that is often served with crispy fries on the side. Head to Café Santiago on Rua de Passos Manuel, where a Francesinha would cost you roughly €10-€12.

Bacalhau à Gomes de Sá is a must-visit for anyone looking for a seaside experience. This classic codfish dish is cooked with potatoes, onions, and olives and topped with hard-boiled eggs. It's a satisfying meal that demonstrates the adaptability of Portugal's famed bacalhau. O Gaveto in Matosinhos serves this meal at a price of roughly €15.

Another local favorite is Tripas à Moda do Porto, a substantial tripe stew dating back to the 15th century. Tripe, white beans, and different meats are used to make this meal, which is both historical and flavorful. Try it at Abadia do Porto on Rua do Ateneu Comercial, where a dish costs about €12–€14.

Bifanas are a popular alternative for those who want a lighter bite. These spicy pork sandwiches are simple yet tasty, frequently served with a cool beer. Conga on Rua do Bonjardim is famed for its bifanas, which cost roughly €3-4 apiece.

Don't miss Caldo Verde, a typical green soup prepared with kale, potatoes, and chorizo. It's a favorite at many local restaurants and ideal for a cold evening. Casa Guedes on Praça dos Poveiros offers a soothing bowl for about €3.

Finally, satiate your sweet taste with Pastel de Nata, the classic Portuguese custard dessert. While they may be found across the nation, Manteigaria on Rua de Alexandre Braga is famous for its freshly baked tarts, which cost roughly €1 apiece.

Top Restaurants and Cafes

When it comes to eating in this quaint Portuguese city, you're in for a treat. The food scene here is bustling, with a variety of classic and modern cuisines to delight your taste buds. Let's check out some of the greatest places to eat or drink coffee.

Begin your day at Café Santiago, a popular restaurant famed for its classic Francesinha, a substantial sandwich that is a local favorite. This café, located on Rua de Passos Manuel, is open daily from midday until 10:45 p.m. Expect to pay between €10 and €15 for a dinner.

Café Majestic on Rua de Santa Catarina is a must-see for anyone seeking an elegant atmosphere. This old café, with its exquisite Art Nouveau décor, provides a window into the past as you have a coffee or a small lunch. It's open from 9 a.m. until 11 p.m. and costs between €15 and €20.

If you're looking for something more international, visit Hard Rock Cafe on Rua Do Almada. This bustling restaurant delivers traditional American cuisine in a rock 'n' roll setting. It's open from 9am until 12:30 a.m., making it ideal for lunch and late-night snacks. Meals here often cost between €20 and €30.

Café Guarany on Avenida dos Aliados offers a more authentic Portuguese experience. This café, known for its live music and colorful environment, is open from 9 a.m. until 11:30 p.m. You can have lunch here for around €15-25.

Each of these establishments provides a distinct flavor of the city's culinary scene, ensuring that your dining experiences are as memorable as the city itself. Whether you want a quick coffee, a full dinner, or a spot to relax with friends, you'll find it here

Local Markets and Food Tours.

When exploring the lovely alleys of this seaside jewel, local markets and cuisine excursions are a must. The bustling Mercado do Bolhão in the center of the city is a sensory feast. This lively market, open from 8 a.m. to 8 p.m. Monday through Saturday, has merchants selling fresh fruit, seafood, meats, and a variety of local specialties. The bustling environment, mixed with the pleasant banter of the stallholders, makes it an ideal location to discover local culture.

For those wishing to delve further into the culinary scene, Taste Porto Food Tours are an excellent choice. These excursions, which start at about €79 per person, provide an immersive taste of the city's culinary treasures. Popular alternatives include the Downtown & Bolhão Market Food Tour. This 3.5-hour trip takes you through the market while also introducing you to lesser-known wine areas and local restaurants. It's a vegetarian and pescatarian-friendly trip, making it suitable for a broad spectrum of cuisine connoisseurs.

If you like craft beer, the Craft Beer & Food Tour is a must-try. This three-hour trip, priced at €69 per person, covers the developing craft beer market, providing insights into the brewing process as well as lots of sampling throughout. It's a refreshing alternative to regular wine excursions, highlighting a distinct aspect of the local beverage culture.

The Food Passport self-guided tour offers a more flexible alternative, allowing you to explore at your speed. This trip costs €40 per person and includes a handpicked selection of must-see destinations, as well as culinary suggestions and cultural insights. It is offered in a variety of languages, making it an ideal option for foreign guests.

Cooking aficionados will like the Porto Cooking Classes, where they can learn to make genuine Portuguese delicacies. These sessions, which cost roughly €125 per person, begin with a market tour to gather fresh ingredients before moving on to the kitchen. It's a hands-on experience that culminates in a fantastic lunch you've made yourself.

Each of these walks provides a unique approach to experiencing the culinary environment, sharing not just cuisine but also the history and traditions that make this city so remarkable. Whether you're eating fresh food at the market or learning the secrets of local dishes, these encounters will leave an indelible impact.

Wine Tasting Experiences

Exploring the wine culture of this seaside city tantalizes the senses. Begin your tour at Graham's Port Lodge, a historic property situated on Rua do Agro 141 in Vila Nova de Gaia. This lodge, open daily from 10 a.m. to 6:30 p.m., provides an in-depth look into the world of Port wine. For roughly €20, you may have a guided tour that includes samples of their best wines, all while admiring the stunning views of the Douro River.

Next, go to Porto Cálem, located at Avenida Diogo Leite 344. This location is open daily from 10 a.m. to 7 p.m. and provides an interactive museum tour followed by a premium wine tasting. The fee is just €15, making it an economical yet engaging experience. The guided tour explains the winemaking process from vineyard to glass and concludes with a tasting session that showcases the distinctive characteristics of their wines.

For a more private atmosphere, de Lima's Wine Bar on Rua Loureiro 69 is an excellent alternative. This small spot, available every day from 3 p.m. to 9 p.m., provides individual wine tastings for up to six people. These experiences, which cost roughly €30 per person, are conducted by skilled presenters who provide tales and insights about each wine, helping you appreciate the local types more.

Lado Wines, situated at Rua Fonte Taurina 89, is another hidden treasure. This location, open from noon to 6 p.m. Monday through Saturday, is devoted to connecting tourists with the wines of the Douro area. For roughly €25, you may attend a tasting session that includes a variety of wines coupled with local cheeses and charcuterie, delivering a well-rounded culinary experience.

Each of these places provides a distinct perspective on the region's rich wine tradition, ensuring that your stay is both instructive and pleasurable. Whether you're a seasoned wine connoisseur or a curious newbie, these encounters will leave you with a greater respect for the local wine culture.

Street Food Guide

The streets are bustling with the smells of sizzling delights, and each turn provides a new culinary experience. Let's go on a gastronomic adventure through busy markets and hidden jewels where residents and tourists alike congregate to indulge in delectable foods.

Begin your day in the ancient Bolhão Market, where traders have been selling fresh food and local delicacies for decades. A pastel de nata, a creamy custard pastry with a flaky crust, costs around €1.50 here. The market is open early at 7 a.m. and closes at 5 p.m., making it an ideal breakfast stop.

As you walk through the small alleyways, you'll see various food carts selling bifana, a typical Portuguese sandwich packed with a seasoned pig. These sandwiches are a deal at just €3 apiece. Conga, situated on Rua do Bonjardim, is a popular place to do this. It is open from 10am to 10pm

For lunch, travel to Ribeiro's riverfront neighborhood and have a francesinha, a hefty sandwich piled with different meats, topped with melted cheese, and drowned in a creamy beer sauce. This sumptuous meal normally costs between €8 and €10. Café Santiago, located on Rua de Passos Manuel, is well-known for offering some of the greatest francesinhas in town. They are open from 11 a.m. to 11 p.m.

In the afternoon, wander around Matosinhos, an area known for its seafood. Grilled sardines, a local specialty, cost about €5. The ideal time to go is at lunchtime, from 12 to 3 p.m. when the seafood is freshest.

As the sun sets, go to Cedofeita, a busy area with a variety of food trucks and pop-up booths. Try the cachorrinho, a spicy hot dog at roughly €4. Gazela, a popular place on Rua de Entre Paredes, is open from 6pm until midnight.

Finish your gastronomic excursion with a sweet treat from one of the many gelato shops spread across the city. A scoop of handcrafted gelato will cost you roughly €2.50. Gelataria Portuense, located on Rua de José Falcão, is popular among residents and remains open until 10 PM.

This city provides a delectable blend of classic tastes and new touches, guaranteeing that each mouthful is an unforgettable experience. So, gather your hunger and discover the delectable street food scene in this charming seaside city.

Cultural Experiences

Festivals & Events

When it comes to festivals and events, this dynamic Portuguese city offers a wealth of cultural opportunities. The calendar is jam-packed with festivals that reflect the rich past and vibrant spirit of its people.

The São João Festival, held annually in June, is a highly anticipated event. This midsummer event is a riot of color and happiness, with both residents and tourists coming to the streets. The night is packed with music, dancing, and a peculiar ritual in which people strike each other on the head with plastic hammers. Fireworks light up the sky, and the fragrance of grilled sardines fills the air, creating a sensory feast.

In September, the city celebrates the Porto Wine Festival, which honors the region's famed port wine. This event is a must-attend for wine connoisseurs since it includes tastings, excursions, and seminars. The event also includes live music and traditional Portuguese food, resulting in an ideal combination of culture and gastronomy.

For music lovers, the Primavera Sound Festival in June is a must-see. This worldwide music festival draws top performers from all over the globe, converting the city into a hotbed of musical talent. The atmosphere is electrifying, with many stages set up across the city, giving a wide selection of genres to satisfy everyone's interests.

The Fantasporto International Film Festival, held in February, is another significant event. This film festival is well-known for its emphasis on the fantasy and science fiction genres, attracting filmmakers and viewers from across the world. Screenings, seminars, and debates make it a refuge for film enthusiasts.

Christmas in this seaside town is a lovely time. The streets are lit up, and the Christmas markets are busy. The markets provide a cheerful shopping experience, with homemade items and delectable food. The main square's large Christmas tree is the focal point, making it an ideal location for holiday photographs.

Throughout the year, the city holds a variety of smaller festivals and events, ranging from jazz music to street art. Each event provides a unique peek into the local culture, making each visit a different experience. Whether you're a gourmet, a music lover, or a cultural buff, there's always something going on in this vibrant city.

Museums & Galleries

Nestled along the Douro River, this bustling Portuguese city is a cultural treasure trove, with museums and galleries that take visitors on a pleasant trip through time and creativity. Let's take a tour of some of the most fascinating places where art and history come to life.

The Serralves Museum of Contemporary Art is first on our list, a contemporary beacon nestled in the verdant Serralves Park. The museum, created by Álvaro Siza Vieira, is a masterpiece in its own right. The shows here are constantly changing, including both Portuguese and foreign artists. The neighboring park, with its tranquil flowers and beautiful sculptures, is an ideal setting for a leisurely walk after seeing the art within.

Next, we visit the National Museum Soares dos Reis, which is situated in the majestic Carrancas Palace. This museum showcases Portugal's rich cultural legacy, with an exceptional collection of paintings, sculptures, and decorative arts. Highlights include pieces by the museum's namesake, 19th-century artist Soares dos Reis, as well as a diverse collection of items from centuries of Portuguese history.

The Portuguese Centre of Photography is a must-see for anybody looking for a unique combination of art and history. This facility, housed in a former jail, provides an intriguing glimpse into the growth of photography in Portugal. The building's towering stone walls and old cells add to the exhibition's allure. This store is a photography enthusiast's dream, with everything from old cameras to current masterpieces.

The Miguel Bombarda Art Block, a dynamic sector full of galleries and creative spaces, is a must-see for art aficionados. You may find the Ó here. Galeria is noted for its emphasis on illustration and graphic art. This gallery is a nexus for rising artists, providing a unique viewpoint on contemporary art.

The region also has several additional galleries, each with its distinct style, making it ideal for a day of gallery hopping.

Another hidden treasure is the Immersive Gallery, which takes a new approach to the classic gallery experience. Located in the ancient Alfândega do Porto, this facility employs cutting-edge technology to produce immersive art experiences. From digital projections to interactive exhibits, the gallery explores new ways to experience art.

The Peculiar Gallery is a must-see for individuals who like the unusual. This gallery, located in the center of the city's art area, features eccentric and unique artwork that defies the norm. It's a place where creativity has no limitations, and each visit brings something new.

Finally, the World of Wine in Vila Nova de Gaia, right over the river, is a cultural complex that extends beyond art. You may visit museums devoted to wine, corks, and even chocolate. It's a sensory trip that blends the region's historic traditions with contemporary displays, making it an excellent complement to any cultural itinerary.

Music and Nightlife

As the sun sets, the city beside the Douro River becomes a playground for night owls and music enthusiasts. The nightlife here is as varied as its old streets, with something for everyone, whether you want to have a quiet drink or dance the night away.

Begin the evening in the Ribeira neighborhood, where cobblestone lanes are dotted with charming pubs and cafés. This area is ideal for a leisurely start to the evening, with the soft hum of conversation and the odd strum of a guitar establishing the tone. Grab a glass of port wine and enjoy the river vista, which is lit by the city's dazzling lights.

Visit a Fado home to experience authentic Portuguese music. These tiny venues provide a look into Portugal's soul via stunningly beautiful music. The vocalists, supported by classical guitars, pour their emotions into every song, creating a mood that is both melancholy and captivating. Casa da Mariquinhas is a popular Fado venue, with music and an environment that transports you to another time.

If you want something more lively, go to Galerias de Paris Street. This vibrant district is teeming with pubs and clubs, each with its distinct flavor. From upscale cocktail bars to subterranean clubs, there are plenty of possibilities. Plano B stands out for its diverse combination of music and art. The facility has many levels and diverse areas that host anything from live bands to DJ performances.

Casa da Música is a must-see destination for live music enthusiasts. This historic music hall accommodates a diverse variety of events, from classical concerts to contemporary shows. The building alone is worth a visit, but the world-class acoustics and diversified program keep visitors coming back. Check the schedule before you go; there is usually something spectacular going on.

If you like comedy, Maus Hábitos provides a combination of stand-up performances and live music. This cultural facility is popular among residents because of its relaxed environment and imaginative programming. Grab a drink, relax, and prepare for an evening of fun and entertainment.

For a more alternative setting, Armazém do Chá is a hidden treasure. This eccentric venue presents a variety of events, including independent bands and electronic music evenings. The diverse design and welcoming atmosphere make it an ideal place to explore new music and dance the night away.

The city's enthusiasm only increases as the night advances. The streets fill up with people, and music can be heard from every corner.

Art & Architecture

Walking through the streets of Portugal's second-largest city, you'll come across a fascinating tapestry of art and architecture spanning many centuries. This city, located on the Douro River, is a UNESCO World Heritage site, and it's simple to understand why. The combination of antique charm and modern innovation produces a visual feast for all visitors.

Begin your adventure in the renowned Casa da Música. This futuristic, diamond-shaped cultural complex, built by Dutch architect Rem Koolhaas, exemplifies the city's innovative spirit. It is more than simply a music venue; it represents contemporary architectural excellence. The building's distinct style and acoustics make it a must-see for architectural aficionados and music fans alike.

Next, go to the Serralves Museum of Contemporary Art. Álvaro Siza Vieira created this museum, which is a remarkable example of modern architecture. The museum is surrounded by magnificent gardens, providing a peaceful getaway from the hustle and bustle of the city. Inside, you'll discover a broad collection of modern art that represents the vibrant cultural landscape.

São Bento Railway Station showcases the city's historical architecture. This station is known for its beautiful azulejo tile panels depicting events from Portuguese history. The complex blue and white tiles are a symbol of the city's artistic legacy, providing a look into its rich history.

Another architectural marvel is the Palácio da Bolsa. This neoclassical edifice, which was previously the city's stock market, has a sumptuous interior, including the famed Arab Room, which was inspired by the Alhambra in Granada. The palace's magnificence and historical importance make it a must-see attraction for every visitor.

Don't miss Livraria Lello, which is widely regarded as one of the world's most beautiful bookshops. Its neo-Gothic façade and gorgeous interior, replete with a grand staircase and stained glass ceiling, make it a must-see for both bookworms and architectural enthusiasts.

As you explore, you'll observe the impact of prominent architects like Álvaro Siza Vieira and Eduardo Souto de Moura, both Pritzker Prize winners. Their creations, such as the Leça Swimming Pools and the Boa Nova Tea House, merge effortlessly into the city's historical fabric, achieving a beautiful mix of old and contemporary.

The city's creative past is not limited to its buildings. Street art and public installations are sprinkled throughout, bringing a dynamic, modern element to the city's ancient streets. The city's public art culture, including murals and sculptures, reflects its creative spirit.

If you're strolling through its ancient Ribeira area with small cobblestone lanes or admiring the contemporary towers that punctuate its skyline, this city provides a thrilling voyage through time and design. Each turn offers a fresh tale, a new work of art, or an architectural marvel, making it a genuinely unique location.

Local Customs and Etiquette

Walking through the lovely alleys of this northern Portuguese city, you'll observe that the residents, known as Tripeiros, have a distinct way of life that is both friendly and welcoming. The folks here are regarded as being forthright. They express themselves freely, and their candor is pleasant. If you ask for directions, don't be shocked if they not only show you around but also recommend a better spot to go.

The São João celebration, held on June 23rd, is a beloved tradition. During this exciting festival, residents strike one other in the head with inflatable hammers and garlic blossoms. It's a unique ritual that draws everyone together in a joyful celebration, filled with laughing and music.

Remember to follow proper dining etiquette. Meals are a leisurely event, therefore it is courteous to wait until everyone has been served before beginning to eat. The people take enormous delight in their food, so enjoy every mouthful of your francesinha or bacalhau. When welcomed to someone's house, it is kind to bring a modest gift, such as flowers or a bottle of wine.

Even if you're meeting someone for the first time, greet them warmly and repeatedly with a kiss on each cheek. This pleasant attitude extends to their hospitality. Don't be shocked if a casual discussion results in an invitation to a family lunch or a local event.

The city's citizens value their traditions and heritage. You'll see it in their festivals, cuisine, and everyday interactions. They are proud of their ancestry and ready to share it with others. So, take the time to interact with them and learn a few Portuguese words; your experience will be enhanced by their real friendliness and openness.

Outdoor Adventures.

Parks and Greenspaces

When you think about Porto, the first thing that comes to mind is probably its ancient architecture, active culture, and, of course, the famed port wine. But, beyond the busy streets and attractive old town, there are plenty of open spots where you may get some fresh air and relax.

Parque da Cidade is one of the most costly and well-loved parks. It is Portugal's biggest urban park, with an area of 83 hectares. Locals throng here for morning jogs, leisurely bike rides, and lakeside picnics. The park's terrain is diversified, including broad grassy fields, woodland regions, and a 10-kilometer network of walkways. The Pavilhão da Água is a scientific museum that explores aquatic life and water-related phenomena. If you want to spend some time on the beach, the park's western side goes right to Praia Internacional's sandy coasts.

Parque de Serralves combines art and nature. This old estate has been turned into a wonderfully landscaped green area complete with formal gardens, forested walks, and open lawns. The park is littered with outdoor sculptures by famous artists such as Claes Oldenburg and Richard Serra. There's also a treetop trek with spectacular views of the park's biodiversity. Serralves also houses Porto's leading modern art museum, making it a cultural hub, particularly during the annual Festa em Serralves in early June.

Another hidden treasure is Porto's Botanical Garden. Despite its tiny size, this botanical garden has a diverse collection of plants. Stroll along small roads past fragrant rose gardens, thorny cactus, and a pond filled with water lilies. The garden's camellias, some of which date back to the nineteenth century, are especially renowned. It's a serene hideaway where you can learn about the region's flora and relax away from the rush and bustle of the city.

If you're looking for a more personal green area, the Crystal Palace Gardens provide spectacular views of the Douro River. The gardens consist of groomed grass, fountains, and meandering walks. It's ideal for a relaxing stroll or a peaceful day with a book. The neighboring Tait House Gardens, with their lush foliage and historic elegance, provide a peaceful getaway.

If you're visiting the city center, don't miss the Cordoaria Gardens. Located near the University of Porto, this park is popular with both students and residents. Its shaded walks, sculptures, and peaceful environment make it an excellent choice for a noon rest.

Each of these parks and gardens provides a distinct experience that highlights the area's natural beauty and cultural depth.

River Activities

The Douro River, which winds through the center of Porto, provides a variety of activities for both adventurers and those wishing to unwind. The river's allure is evident, with its picturesque sights and lively environment.

Begin your adventure with a peaceful sail down the Douro. These excursions provide a unique view of the city's ancient buildings, including the famed Dom Luís I Bridge. As you float down the water, you'll pass through the vibrant Ribeira neighborhood, where houses seem to fall to the riverbed. The excursions often feature a guide who tells intriguing anecdotes about the city's history and relationship to the river.

For those who want a more active vacation, kayaking on the Douro is an excellent choice. Paddling along the calm waters allows you to discover secret nooks and get close to the riverbanks. It's a relaxing way to appreciate the natural beauty of the region while getting some exercise. Kayak rentals are accessible at many locations along the river, making it simple to go on this trip.

If you're looking for something a little more exciting, consider stand-up paddleboarding. This pastime has gained popularity in recent years and is a great way to traverse the river. Balancing on the board while paddling gives you a full-body exercise as well as a unique view of the surroundings. There are various locations along the river where you can rent paddle boards and even get a lesson if you're new to the sport.

The Douro River is a fantastic fishing destination. The river is home to a variety of fish species, and local guides can show you the finest fishing places. Whether you're an experienced fisherman or a novice, spending a day fishing on the Douro is a pleasant way to reconnect with nature.

A sunset cruise offers a very unique experience. As the sun sets below the horizon, the river takes on a magnificent appearance. The sky is painted in shades of orange and pink, which reflect off the lake and create a gorgeous image. Many of these cruises include wine tastings, which enable you to try some of the region's famed port wines while admiring the breathtaking scenery.

No trip to the Douro River is complete without visiting the wine cellars at Vila Nova de Gaia, right across the river. You may learn about the history of port wine manufacturing and try some of the best kinds. The cellars are a short walk from the riverside, making it simple to combine a river excursion with a wine-tasting tour.

Day Trips from Porto.

Porto, with its lively culture and spectacular architecture, serves as an excellent base for visiting northern Portugal's lush landscapes and medieval villages. Whether you like history, wildlife, or wine, there is a day excursion that will appeal to your senses.

Douro Valley

The Douro Valley, a short train trip from the city, is a must-see for everyone who enjoys magnificent landscapes and world-class wine. The valley, a UNESCO World Heritage site, is known for its terraced vineyards that produce the famed Port wine. Take a leisurely sail down the Douro River to enjoy the stunning views and see quaint communities like Pinhão. Many vineyards provide tours and tastings, allowing you to experience some of the greatest wines in the area.

Braga

Braga, sometimes known as the "Rome of Portugal," is one of the country's oldest and most historically significant cities. The city is home to the beautiful Bom Jesus do Monte, a baroque church built on a hill with a grand stairway. Wander around the old district, where you'll discover picturesque squares, antique churches, and a bustling atmosphere. Braga is conveniently accessible by rail, making it an ideal day vacation.

Guimarães

This city, known Portugal's birthplace, is a medieval city with a rich history. The old center is a UNESCO World Heritage site, with tiny alleys, charming squares, and well-preserved buildings. Visit Guimarães Castle and the Palace of the Dukes of Braganza to learn about the country's history. The city is just a short train journey from Porto, allowing for a convenient and pleasant day excursion.

Aveiro

It is nicknamed the "Venice of Portugal," is well-known for its canals and colorful moliceiro boats. Stroll along the canals, see the Art Nouveau structures, and try the local specialty, ovos moles. The adjacent Costa Nova beach, with its distinctive striped buildings, is well worth a visit. Aveiro is readily accessible by rail, making it an ideal day excursion for anyone wishing to see another side of Portugal.

National Park of Peneda-Gerês.

For nature lovers, a visit to Parque Nacional da Peneda-Gerês is essential. This national park has breathtaking scenery, ranging from harsh mountains to peaceful lakes and waterfalls. Hiking routes abound, allowing you to explore the rich flora and animals. The park is a little farther away, therefore hiring a vehicle is advisable to properly appreciate the natural splendor of the region.

Matosinhos

If you're searching for a beach vacation, travel to Matosinhos. This coastal resort is well-known for its broad sandy beaches and superb seafood eateries. It's a popular surfing destination, and there are lots of surf schools to try. Matosinhos is just a short metro ride from the city, providing a convenient and enjoyable day excursion.

Each of these sites provides a distinct perspective on northern Portugal's rich beauty and culture. Whether you're seeing ancient sites, sampling world-renowned wines, or trekking through breathtaking scenery, there's a day excursion from Porto that will leave you with lasting memories.

Beach Escapes

When you think of a beach getaway in this quaint Portuguese city, your thoughts may not immediately turn to its sandy coastlines. However, this coastal jewel provides a beautiful assortment of beach cottages that are just a tram ride from the busy city center.

Begin your tour in Praia dos Ingleses, a beach renowned for its golden sands and rocky outcrops. Located in the upmarket Foz do Douro area, this location is ideal for a leisurely walk along the waterfront promenade. The cafés here are a highlight, keeping up late into the night, making it an ideal location to relax with a drink as the sun goes down.

Praia do Carneiro is a short distance away, at the mouth of the River Douro. This beach is distinguished by the historic breakwater and the Farol de Felgueiras lighthouse. While the sand may not be the softest, the historical background of the 16th-century Fortaleza de São João da Foz gives a distinct flavor to the visit.

Praia de Matosinhos offers a more typical beach experience. This broad length of excellent golden sand is popular with both residents and tourists. It's a bustling location where you can watch surfers and play beach soccer. The adjacent Matosinhos municipal market is ideal for purchasing fresh fish to eat by the water.

If you're looking for a quick excursion, drive south to Miramar. This little coastal hamlet is notable for the Capela do Senhor A Pedra, a 17th-century church located on a rocky cliff. The beach here, Praia de Miramar, provides a peaceful respite with its exposed but nice beaches.

Another hidden beauty on the shore is Praia do Molhe. It has a combination of coarse sand and boulders, as do its nearby beaches. The stone jetty stretching from the beach is a unique feature that creates a gorgeous backdrop for a day by the water.

Each of these beaches has its distinct charm and vibe, making them ideal for a day excursion or a peaceful afternoon away from the city's hustle and bustle. Whether you want to soak up the sun, take a refreshing plunge in the Atlantic, or just enjoy the coastal vistas, these seaside getaways will leave you with unforgettable memories.

Shopping in Porto.

Souvenir Ideas

Wandering around the picturesque alleyways of this northern Portuguese jewel, you'll discover a treasure trove of one-of-a-kind mementos that reflect the soul of your trip. Let's look at some of the greatest souvenirs you can bring home.

Begin with the renowned port wine. This fortified wine, made solely in the Douro Valley, is a must-buy. Visit the cellars of Vila Nova de Gaia, right over the river, to taste and buy bottles from famous producers like Taylor's, Graham's, and Sandeman. Prices vary but expect to spend between €10 and €30 for a nice bottle.

Arcádia chocolates are a delicious treat. This ancient confectionery, situated in the center of the city, has been making chocolate since 1933. Their variety ranges from basic truffles to innovative tastes influenced by local delicacies. A package of these delightful delicacies is normally priced between €5 and €20.

If you're searching for something really Portuguese, try purchasing some handcrafted tile jewelry. These sculptures, inspired by the gorgeous azulejos seen on many buildings, create exquisite and one-of-a-kind presents. They may be found in numerous artisan stores across the city, with costs ranging from €10 to €50 depending on the complexity of the design.

A linen or cotton home textile is an excellent keepsake. The north of Portugal is famed for its high-quality textiles, and businesses like Casa Dos Linhos sell a broad variety of items, from tablecloths to bedding. Located near the Bolhão Market, this boutique offers finely created products that will remind you of your vacation every time. Prices vary but expect to spend between €20 and €100 depending on the item.

Canned sardines are a traditional Portuguese product that provides a flavor of the sea. Shops like Conserveira do Bolhão at the Mercado do Bolhão provide a choice of tastes and packaging options. These make for a unique and tasty keepsake, with costs ranging from €3 to €10 per can.

Claus Porto's artisanal soaps are another luxury alternative. Founded in 1887, this company is well-known for its elegantly packaged, high-quality soaps and toiletries. Their boutique on Rua das Flores has a variety of perfumes and items, ideal for treating yourself or someone special. A bar of soap is normally priced between €10 and €20.

Don't forget to buy some local coffee. Pérola do Bolhão, situated on Rua Formosa, has been offering the city's best coffee beans since 1917. You may buy a variety of mixes and roasts to take home, with costs ranging from €5 to €15 per bag.

Local Markets.

Strolling around this northern Portuguese city's lively marketplaces is a sensory-rich experience. Each market provides a unique peek into local culture, offering a wide selection of items from fresh vegetables to handcrafted crafts.

Begin your adventure in Mercado do Bolhão, a historic market on Rua Formosa. This lively establishment has been a fixture since 1914, serving everything from fresh fruits and vegetables to meats, cheeses, and baked delicacies. Monday through Friday, 8 a.m. to 8 p.m.; Saturday, 8 a.m. to 6 p.m. It is closed on Sundays and holidays. Prices here are fairly affordable, with fresh vegetables often costing less than in supermarkets.

Next, visit Mercado Beira-Rio, located on Avenida Ramos Pinto in Vila Nova de Gaia. This market blends traditional vendors with contemporary cafes, making it an excellent location to try local cuisine. It's open every day from 11 a.m. to 10 p.m., making it ideal for a relaxing afternoon visit. Everything from fresh seafood to gourmet pastries is available, with costs changing depending on what you're looking for.

For a more diversified experience, go to Porto Belo Market on Praça de Carlos Alberto. This market is open every Saturday from 10 a.m. to 7 p.m. and is filled with antique things, vinyl records, and handcrafted crafts. It's a terrific location to discover unusual souvenirs and presents, with costs ranging from a few euros for modest items to much more for uncommon treasures.

Another must-see destination is the Clérigos Market on Rua de Cândido dos Reis. This market is well-known for its antiques and odd things, making it popular among collectors. It is open on weekends and is a great spot to spend a few hours looking through old books, antique clothes, and other interesting items. Prices vary greatly, so be prepared to negotiate a little.

For those looking for fresh, local goods, the Super Talho O Barroso in Rua do Amial is an excellent option. This market is open Monday through Friday from 7:30 AM to 8 PM and Saturdays till 7 PM. It sells high-quality meats and other fresh items. It's a little off the main route, but it's well worth a visit for its real local character.

Also visit the Mercado Bom Sucesso, a contemporary market situated near the Boavista roundabout. This market has been rejuvenated in recent years, with a mix of traditional food vendors and fashionable restaurants. It's open every day from 10 a.m. to 11 p.m. and is an excellent spot to dine while shopping for fresh fruit, artisanal cheeses, and other gourmet things. Prices here are somewhat higher, reflecting the market's upmarket atmosphere.

Each of these markets provides a distinct glimpse into local life, making them must-see destinations for anybody visiting this charming city. Happy shopping!

Boutique and Artisan Shops

Begin your tour with Coração Alecrim, a charming store situated on Rua do Rosário 274. This eco-friendly boutique has a carefully chosen range of sustainable clothes, home décor, and antique products. The warm, friendly ambiance makes it ideal for discovering one-of-a-kind artifacts that tell a narrative. Open from 11 a.m. to 7 p.m., it's a paradise for folks who value smart design and ethical buying.

Next, go to Claus Porto at Rua das Flores 22. This legendary business, which opened in 1887, is known for its luxury soaps and scents. The décor, with marble countertops and classic furnishings, takes you to another period. Prices for their nicely wrapped soaps start at about €10, making them ideal presents or souvenirs. The store is open every day from 10 a.m. until 8 p.m.

A Vida Portuguesa, located in Rua Galeria de Paris 20, offers a sample of local creativity. This store highlights Portuguese history with a diverse selection of traditional goods, including pottery and textiles. Each piece is carefully chosen to represent the country's rich cultural heritage. Open from 10 a.m. to 8 p.m., it is a must-see for everyone wishing to bring a bit of Portugal home.

The Feeting Room in Rua do Bolhão 55 offers a modern and stylish atmosphere. This concept shop features new designers and sells a variety of clothes, accessories, and lifestyle items. The shop's basic decor creates an ideal background for the creative things on show. It's open from 11 a.m. to 8 p.m. and is an excellent place to learn about current trends.

Don't miss Mercado do Bolhão, a traditional market on Rua Formosa. While it is well renowned for its fresh vegetables and local delights, it also has vendors offering handcrafted crafts and artisanal products. The market's bustling ambiance and unique mix of sellers make it an exciting place to explore. It's open from 7 a.m. to 5 p.m. and is a great location to learn about local culture and purchase unique items.

Then, try going to Livraria Lello at Rua das Carmelitas 144. Though largely a bookshop, its gorgeous architecture and historical charm make it a must-see. The business also sells lovely stationery and interesting presents. Open from 9:30 a.m. to 7 p.m., it's a magnificent setting that has inspired many, including J.K. Rowling during her stay in the city.

Each of these stores provides a unique experience, reflecting the rich and colorful culture of this stunning seaside city.

Best Shopping Streets

When it comes to shopping in this bustling Portuguese city, a few streets stand out due to their distinct goods and energetic ambiance.

Rua de Santa Catarina is the center of retail therapy. This lively boulevard is dotted with a mix of multinational names like Zara and H&M, as well as quaint local stores. The route is pedestrian-friendly, making it ideal for a relaxing walk while shopping. Don't miss the renowned Café Majestic, the ideal place to rest your feet and sip a coffee. Most stores open about 10 a.m. and shut around 7 p.m., while some bigger stores may remain open until 9 p.m. Prices range greatly, from inexpensive fashion discoveries to more premium products.

For a more traditional shopping experience, visit Rua das Flores. This charming boulevard is famous for its handmade businesses and local crafts. You may get one-of-a-kind jewelry, handcrafted leather products, and traditional

Portuguese pottery. The mood is more casual than in crowded Santa Catarina, and it's a terrific spot to discover unique items. Shops normally open at 10 a.m. and shut around 8 p.m. Prices might vary from a few euros for tiny trinkets to more for artisan products.

Rua de Miguel Bombarda is the go-to spot for art enthusiasts. This street is well-known for its modern art galleries and offbeat stores. It serves as a focus for the creative community, with several boutiques displaying the work of local artists and designers. The street also offers frequent art events and exhibits, making it a lively destination to visit. Most galleries and businesses open at 11 a.m. and shut around 7 p.m. Prices here may be exorbitant due to the unique and frequently personalized nature of the things available.

For those seeking luxury, Avenida da Boavista provides high-end retail in a more contemporary atmosphere. This route is lined with fashionable shops and high-end retailers, ideal for visitors eager to indulge. The region also has various gourmet restaurants and trendy cafés, making it an ideal destination to spend the whole day. Shops normally open at 10 a.m. and shut at 8 p.m., with some remaining open later. Prices here are greater, attracting a more upscale audience.

Each of these alleys represents a distinct aspect of the city's retail environment, ranging from high-street fashion to unique local crafts and luxury products. Whether you're searching for a bargain or a unique remembrance, there's something for everyone.

Online Shopping Tips

Shopping online in this attractive Portuguese city may be a pleasant experience if you know where to search and what to expect. Here are some pointers to help you have a seamless and pleasurable online buying experience.

When it comes to discovering unique local items, many craftsmen and small companies have embraced the Internet revolution. Websites such as A Vida Portuguesa provide a carefully chosen variety of traditional Portuguese products, ranging from soaps and pottery to gourmet meals.

Prices vary, but products may range from €10 for little trinkets to more than €100 for intricate sculptures. Delivery timeframes are usually within a week, however, you should always verify the projected delivery date before making an order.

El Corte Inglés is a popular online department store among fashion fans. It has a diverse selection of apparel, accessories, and cosmetic goods from both foreign and local companies. The website is easy to use, and specials and discounts are often available. Prices vary from reasonable to high-end, depending on the brand. They provide a variety of delivery choices, including rapid delivery for last-minute orders.

If you're seeking for electronics or household appliances, Worten is a trusted source. This well-known shop provides a full online store where you can buy anything from the most recent smartphones to kitchen appliances.
Prices are competitive, and they often run deals. The majority of things arrive within a few days after ordering. They also provide a click-and-collect option if you want to pick up your item in person.

Fnac is a bookworm's paradise. Their online shop offers an extensive assortment of books, music, and technology. The prices are low, and they usually have special deals. Delivery timeframes vary, however, most purchases are completed within one week. They also have a membership program, which provides extra savings and privileges.

When purchasing online, you should be aware of the return rules. Most respectable retailers have clear return policies, but it is always a good idea to check the tiny print. Also, keep a watch out for delivery expenses, since they may pile up, particularly if you're shopping from many shops.

Continente provides a comprehensive online grocery service for people who want to buy from the comfort of their own homes. You may purchase anything from fresh food to home necessities. Prices are similar to in-store buying, and they provide a variety of delivery times to accommodate your schedule. Delivery costs are typically approximately €5, however they often provide deals that lower or remove this cost.

Accommodation Options

Types of Accommodations

When selecting somewhere to stay in this attractive Portuguese city, there are several possibilities for every taste and budget. From opulent hotels to modest guesthouses, each form of lodging provides a distinct experience.

For those wanting a touch of refinement, the InterContinental Palacio das Cardosas is an excellent alternative. This five-star hotel, built in a magnificently renovated 18th-century palace, is in the heart of the historic district. Guests may enjoy large accommodations with breathtaking views, as well as a fitness facility and spa. Prices begin at about €250 per night, making it an upscale choice for a special occasion.

If modern luxury is more your thing, the Sheraton Hotel & Spa provides a contemporary experience with all of the facilities you could want. This hotel, located in the Boavista neighborhood, has a well-equipped fitness center, a relaxing spa, and an on-site restaurant. Rooms here start at around €200 per night.

For budget-conscious tourists, the Poet's Inn offers a pleasant and economical solution. This guesthouse, located in the Bonfim area, provides pleasant accommodations and a welcoming ambiance. The prices are pretty affordable, beginning at about €50 per night. It's an excellent choice for anyone wishing to explore the local scene without breaking the wallet.

Hostels are also a popular alternative, particularly among younger tourists and those wishing to meet new people. The Passenger Hostel, situated in the lively Ribeira sector, stands out. With its active social scene and clean, pleasant dormitories, it's ideal for individuals who want to be right in the heart of things. Beds in shared dormitories start from €20 per night.

For a more personal experience, try staying at a boutique hotel such as Casa da Companhia. This magnificent choice, situated on Rua das Flores, combines traditional elegance with contemporary comfort. It's a relaxing oasis, complete with an indoor and outdoor pool, sauna, and wellness center. Prices here start at about €349 per night.

The Best Neighborhoods to Stay

Ribeira, the historic heart, is popular with first-time tourists. This region, with its colorful houses and small medieval lanes, is along the Douro River and provides breathtaking views and a bustling environment. The Pestana Vintage Porto Hotel, situated on the riverbank, offers a magnificent stay with rooms beginning at €200 per night. The neighborhood is buzzing with cafés, restaurants, and bars, making it an excellent alternative for individuals who want to be in the thick of the action.

You can also visit Bonfim, an up-and-coming district noted for its artsy ambiance and hipster cafés. This region is somewhat off the beaten road while still near to the major attractions. Charming guest houses, such as the Poet's Inn, provide accommodations starting at about €50 per night. Bonfim has a more casual environment, ideal for those who want to see the city like a native.

Cedofeita is the destination for stylish nightlife and modern art. This neighborhood is home to Rua de Miguel Bombarda, which is famous for its art galleries and concept businesses. The Gallery Hostel, situated in this creative district, provides both private and dorm rooms, with rates beginning at €25 per night. Cedofeita's dynamic nightlife and artistic spirit make it a popular destination for young travelers and art lovers.

If you're traveling with family, Boavista is an excellent choice. This residential region is calmer and more expansive, with several parks and green areas. The Sheraton Hotel & Spa in Boavista provides a comfortable stay with family-friendly features including a pool and wellness center. Rooms here start at around €200 per night. Boavista's tranquil atmosphere makes it suitable for families seeking a relaxing escape.

For wine enthusiasts, Vila Nova de Gaia is the ideal neighborhood. Located close to the river, this neighborhood is well-known for its port wine cellars. Staying here provides convenient access to wine tastings and excursions. The

Yeatman Hotel, a premium wine hotel, has breathtaking views of the city and river. Rooms start at about €300 per night, and the hotel has a Michelin-starred restaurant and a large wine cellar.

Budget versus Luxury Stays

There are a variety of alternatives available, when it comes to selecting somewhere to stay in this charming Portuguese city, from budget-friendly jewels to lavish getaways, each with its own distinct experience.

If you're visiting on a budget, the Moov Hotel Porto Norte is an excellent alternative. This hotel in Matosinhos provides a pleasant and casual environment. Rooms are functional and pleasant, with standard facilities like soundproofing, flat-screen televisions, and eco-friendly showers. Prices start at about €50 per night, making it a great choice for budget-conscious tourists. The hotel is strategically located near the Sete Bicas Metro Station, allowing quick access to the city center.

The Poet's Inn, located in the Bonfim area, is another excellent cheap alternative. This guesthouse provides a comfortable and inviting atmosphere, with rooms beginning at about €50 per night. It's ideal for people who want to soak in the local atmosphere without breaking the bank. The region is noted for its artsy vibe and hipster cafés, which provide a more laid-back experience.

Luxury travelers will find the InterContinental Palacio das Cardosas an excellent option. This five-star hotel, built in a magnificently renovated 18th-century palace, is in the heart of the historic district. Guests may enjoy large accommodations with breathtaking views, as well as a fitness facility and spa. Prices begin at about €250 per night, making it an upscale choice for a special occasion. The hotel's prime position puts you only steps away from the city's biggest attractions.

The Sheraton Hotel & Spa in the Boavista neighborhood provides a modern luxury experience with all of the facilities you could want. This hotel has a well-equipped fitness club, a relaxing spa, and an on-site restaurant. Rooms here start at around €200 per night. Boavista's gentler, residential ambiance makes it suitable for those looking for a relaxing getaway.

For an even more luxurious stay, visit the Yeatman Hotel in Vila Nova de Gaia. This luxurious wine hotel has breathtaking views of both the city and the Douro River. Rooms start at about €300 per night, and the hotel has a Michelin-starred restaurant and a large wine cellar. Staying here provides you quick access to the famed port wine cellars, which are ideal for wine connoisseurs.

Whether you want to economize or spend, this city has a variety of lodgings to fit every budget and style. This colorful and historic location offers something for everyone, from budget-friendly hotels and guesthouses to exquisite getaways.

Booking Tips

When planning your vacation to this attractive Portuguese city, arranging your accommodations and activities ahead of time might make a big impact. The city, noted for its ancient architecture and dynamic culture, has a wide range of lodging and activities to suit diverse interests and budgets.

Staying in the Ribeira region offers a genuinely immersive experience. This region, with its scenic riverside and ancient alleyways, is designated a UNESCO World Heritage Site. Hotels here, such as the Pestana Vintage Porto, provide breathtaking views of the Douro River. Prices may vary between €150 and €300 per night, depending on the season. Booking a hotel well in advance is recommended, particularly during the peak season of May to September.

If you want a more central location, the Aliados neighborhood is perfect. Many of the city's most popular attractions are located in this region, including the historic Livraria Lello and the Clérigos Tower. The InterContinental Porto - Palacio das Cardosas, housed in a magnificently renovated 18th-century palace, has luxurious rooms for about €200 per night. For a more affordable choice, try the PortoBay Hotel Teatro, where accommodations start at about €100 per night.

Foz do Douro is an excellent alternative for individuals who appreciate being by the shore. This area, situated near the Atlantic Ocean, has a more casual atmosphere. The Hotel Boa-Vista, with its rooftop pool and ocean views, is a popular option. Prices here start at about €120 per night. It's a 40-minute bus or tram journey from the city center, making it a handy yet relaxing alternative.

When it comes to eating, Porto has an abundance of fantastic eateries. For a memorable night out, book a reservation at Antiqvvm, a Michelin-starred restaurant that serves superb Portuguese food. It's an unforgettable dining experience, housed in a historic structure with breathtaking views of the Douro River. Expect to spend around €100 per person.

Reservations should be made several weeks in advance, particularly during the busy tourist season.

For a more relaxed eating experience, visit the Mercado do Bolhão. This ancient market, open from 8 a.m. to 8 p.m., is a perfect spot to try local specialties like bifana (a traditional pig sandwich) and pastel de nata (a popular Portuguese custard pastry). Prices are relatively affordable, with most snacks costing less than €5.

Getting about the city is simple with the Andante Card, which costs €0.60 and comes preloaded with credit for usage on the metro and buses. The metro system runs efficiently and links many sections of the city, including the airport. Trams like the Funicular dos Guindais provide gorgeous rides and are enjoyable ways to visit the sites. Tram tickets cost €3.50 one-way, while the funicular trip costs the same amount.

Booking your activities ahead of time might help you make the most of your trip. A must-do is the Six Bridges Cruise on the Douro River, which provides a unique viewpoint on the city's architecture and history. Tickets for the trip start at about €15 and may be purchased online or at the dock.

Consider taking a tour of Vila Nova de Gaia's port wine cellars to get a feel for the local culture. Many of the cellars, like Sandeman and Graham's, provide guided tours and tastings. Prices vary but expect to spend approximately €20 for a tour and sampling session. These trips are popular, so it is best to book in advance.

Planning ahead of time and making arrangements as needed will guarantee a smooth and pleasurable vacation to this wonderful city. Whether you stay in the historic district, on the sea, or anywhere in between, there is something for everyone in this lively and inviting city.

Unique Places to Stay

The InterContinental Porto - Palacio das Cardosas is located in the city's historic core. This five-star hotel is set in a magnificently renovated 18th-century castle and has large rooms with spectacular views of the city's attractions. Prices start at about €200 per night, and the hotel's central position gives it an excellent base for visiting the surrounding sights.

For a touch of luxury, **the Maison Albar - le Monumental Palace** is an excellent alternative. This five-star hotel in the city center has a grandiose design, a Michelin-starred restaurant, and a peaceful spa. Rooms here start at about €250 per night, and the hotel's exquisite atmosphere and excellent service make for an unforgettable stay.

If you're searching for something a little more unique, **the M Maison Particulière Porto** provides a boutique experience in a 16th-century property. This hotel in the old town has a traditional Parisian air, with magnificent rooms decorated with great art and antiques. Prices vary, so check availability and pricing online.

Armazém Luxury Housing offers a one-of-a-kind architectural experience. This boutique hotel is housed in a 19th-century iron warehouse in the historic district. The elegant rooms and flats are created with an emphasis on interior design, providing a mix of industrial vibes and contemporary comfort. Prices start at about €150 per night, and the hotel's terrace offers spectacular views of the city.

In the Ribeira area, **the InPatio Guest House** provides a pleasant accommodation with views of a tiny patio. This hostel is a short walk from the Palácio da Bolsa and the Porto Cathedral. Rooms are individually decorated, with some having stone walls or designer furnishings. Prices start at about €100 per night, making it an excellent choice for people seeking a comfortable and reasonable stay.

For a beach getaway, **the Hotel Boa-Vista in Foz do Douro** is an excellent option. This hotel's rooftop pool with ocean views provides a quiet getaway from the hustle and bustle of the city center. Prices start at about €120 per night, and the hotel's position near the Atlantic Ocean creates a relaxing ambiance.

Booking your accommodation in advance is usually a smart idea, particularly during the peak season of May to September. Whether you want elegance, charm, or a one-of-a-kind architectural experience, this fascinating city has something for everyone.

Understanding Local Laws and Customs

Essential Legal Information

Navigating the legal environment in Porto is simple if you understand what to anticipate. Whether you're planning a short vacation or a longer stay, knowing the local regulations may make your stay easier and more pleasant.

First and foremost, always carry a proper ID. Portuguese law requires you to carry identification at all times. If you are a citizen of the European Union, this may be your passport or national identification card. If you are driving, you must have a driver's license, and if it is not from an EU country, you may need an International Driving Permit.

Speaking about driving, the laws of the road in Porto are comparable to those across Europe. Seat belts are required for all passengers, and using a cell phone while driving is completely forbidden unless you have a hands-free device. Speed restrictions are strictly enforced, with urban areas normally capped at 50 km/h and highways at 120 km/h. Parking might be difficult in the city center, so check for authorized parking spots to avoid penalties.

Public transit is effective and frequently utilized. If you're taking a bus or tram, verify your ticket as soon as you board. Failure to do so may result in significant penalties. The metro system is also a good method to get about, but be sure you have a valid ticket.

The legal drinking age for alcohol is 18 years old. Drinking in public areas is typically discouraged, and there are stringent regulations against drinking and driving. The blood alcohol level is 0.05%, and exceeding it carries harsh consequences, including substantial fines and jail.

Smoking is prohibited in enclosed public venues, such as restaurants, bars, and public transportation. If you need to light up, check for the approved smoking places.

If you're renting an apartment or staying at a hotel, be mindful of the noise rules. Quiet hours are normally from 11pm to 7am, and excessive noise during these periods may result in complaints and penalties.

Those wishing to work or study in Porto should verify they have the appropriate visas and permissions. Starting early is recommended since the procedure might be long. If you are working, your employer should help with the paperwork. Students will have to communicate with their school institution.

Porto has good healthcare choices, both public and private. EU nationals may use their European Health Insurance Card (EHIC) to obtain public healthcare. If you are not from the European Union, you should have full travel insurance.

Finally, be aware of your surroundings and personal things. Porto is largely safe, however, like with any big city, small crime does occur. Keep a watch on your possessions, particularly in busy locations and tourist attractions.

Health and Safety Guidelines

Porto, with its lovely streets and dynamic culture, is a wonderful vacation, but it's always a good idea to follow health and safety precautions to guarantee a safe journey.

Porto's healthcare is good, with both public and private facilities providing high-quality treatment. EU nationals may use their European Health Insurance Card (EHIC) to access public healthcare, however, non-EU tourists should have complete travel insurance. Pharmacies are ubiquitous and well-stocked, often marked with a green cross, and many are open 24 hours.

Staying healthy in Porto requires a few easy steps. Tap water is safe to drink, however bottled water is easily accessible if desired. The city has a pleasant temperature, although summers can be extremely hot, so keeping hydrated and using sunscreen is crucial. If you have any special health concerns, you should see your doctor before visiting.

Safety in Porto is normally not a problem, since the city is regarded as one of Europe's safest locations. However, like in any metropolitan region, it is essential to be attentive. Petty crime, such as pickpocketing, may occur, particularly in busy tourist areas and on public transportation. Keep your possessions safe, and exercise caution with your valuables.

Public transit is dependable and safe, but keep a watch on your personal belongings. To prevent problems, employ only licensed taxi services. Walking about Porto is enjoyable, but be aware of uneven footpaths and cobblestone streets, which may be problematic, particularly after rain.

Emergency services in Porto are efficient and may be accessed via 112. This number will link you to police, fire, and medical services. It's a good idea to store this number on your phone just in case.

Those intending to drive should be advised that traffic might be congested, and parking in the city center is typically difficult. Always wear a seatbelt and avoid using your phone while driving. Speed restrictions are severely enforced, with urban areas averaging 50 km/h and highways reaching 120 km/h.

Porto is an excellent city to visit, with a rich history, gorgeous architecture, and delectable food. Following these health and safety recommendations will allow you to enjoy all this wonderful city has to offer in peace.

Local Transportation Regulations

Once you've figured out how to use Porto's transit system, it's easy to navigate. The city provides a range of transportation alternatives, each with its unique beauty and ease.

The Metro is popular with both residents and tourists. With six lines and 81 stops, it serves a large portion of the city and its suburbs. The Metro runs from 6 a.m. to 1 a.m., giving it a consistent alternative for most of the day. Tickets are moderately affordable, with a single ride costing between €1.20 and €2.00, depending on which zones you go through. Tickets may be purchased at machines in the stations and must be validated before boarding.

Buses provided by STCP are another important component of Porto's public transportation system. These blue and white buses traverse the city, going where the Metro does not. A single bus ticket costs around €2.00 and may be purchased straight from the driver. Please remember to verify your ticket as soon as you board. The buses operate from early morning to late at night, although timetables vary, so check the itinerary ahead of time.

Take a ride on one of Porto's old trams for a nostalgic experience. These beautiful automobiles have been rattling about the streets since the early twentieth century. There are three primary tram lines, the most picturesque being Line 1, which runs along the riverbank. A single tram journey costs €3.50, and tickets may be bought onboard.

The Funicular dos Guindais provides a unique mode of transportation between the Ribeira neighborhood and Batalha. This short but hilly ride offers breathtaking views of the Douro River and the city. A one-way ticket costs €2.50, and the funicular runs every day from 8 a.m. to 10 p.m.

Taxis are available and reasonably priced in Porto. They may be hailed on the street, discovered at taxi stands, or reserved by phone or app. The basic ticket is roughly €3.25, with extra charges per kilometer and for baggage. Taxis are a practical choice, particularly late at night or when traveling to locations not well-serviced by public transportation.

For individuals who desire greater freedom, ride-sharing services such as Uber are accessible in Porto. Prices are similar to taxis, and the ease of reserving via an app makes it a popular option.

Cycling is gaining popularity in Porto, with more bike lanes and rental alternatives available. Helmets are not required, however, they are advised for safety. Follow traffic regulations and use designated bike lanes whenever feasible.

If you intend to use public transportation regularly, consider purchasing a Porto Card or an Andante Tour card. These passes provide unrestricted access to the Metro, buses, and certain regional trains, as well as discounts at numerous attractions. The Porto Card also provides free admission to various museums and monuments, making it an excellent bargain for visitors.

Social norms

Porto's social standards are a fusion of ancient Portuguese practices and the city's distinct identity. The people here are recognized for their friendliness and kindness, which make tourists feel right at home.

It's always nice to greet someone with a cheerful "Bom dia" (Good morning) or "Boa tarde". When meeting someone for the first time, a handshake is standard, but among friends and relatives, it is normal to exchange two kisses on the cheeks, beginning with the right.

Dining etiquette is crucial. Meals are occasions for mingling, and it is courteous to wait until everyone has been served before beginning to eat. If you're invited to someone's house, bringing a little gift, such as flowers or a bottle of wine, is a kind gesture. During meals, keep your hands visible but not touching the table, and use utensils for most dishes, including fruit.

Dress standards are relatively flexible, however it is advisable to dress formally while eating out or visiting more affluent venues. Beachwear should only be worn on the beach, and modest apparel is preferred while visiting churches or religious locations.

Public shows of love are widespread and usually welcomed, but you should be aware of your surroundings. In more conservative circumstances, it's best to remain discreet.

Tipping is usual, but not required. In restaurants, a tip of 5-10% of the bill is customary if the service is satisfactory. It is a kind gesture for taxi drivers and hotel workers to round up the fee or leave a tiny tip.

There is a casual attitude to timeliness. Arriving a few minutes late is typically not an issue, but it's always polite to notify someone if you'll be considerably delayed.

Respect for personal space is important, yet people here are also quite tactile. Don't be shocked if someone touches your arm during a discussion; it indicates friendship.

Giving up your seat for the elderly, pregnant women, or those with impairments is considered good public transit etiquette. Speaking quietly on your phone and keeping your stuff close to prevent obstructing the aisle are also smart habits.

Smoking is not permitted in enclosed public locations, including restaurants and bars unless there is a designated smoking spot. It is courteous to get permission before lighting up in someone's house or proximity to others.

Understanding these social conventions will help you fit in and enjoy your stay in this bustling city. The residents' genuine warmth and laid-back attitude make it simple to feel at ease and fully immerse yourself in the culture.

Emergency Contacts

Knowing who to contact in an emergency might mean all the difference. Portugal's main emergency number is 112, which links you to medical services, the fire department, and the police. This line is free to call from any phone and runs 24 hours a day, seven days a week, guaranteeing that support is always accessible.

For non-emergency health needs, the Saúde 24 line is a great resource. Dial 808 24 24 24 for medical consultation and help at any time of day. This service is especially beneficial for non-urgent health concerns since it provides peace of mind without the need for a hospital visit.

If you want police help, the Public Security Police (PSP) handle urban areas, whilst the National Republican Guard (GNR) handles rural areas. Both troops are committed to ensuring safety and order. You may contact the PSP directly in Porto by dialing 222 077 500.

In the unfortunate case of a fire, the Bombeiros (firefighters) are well-trained and prepared to react. They may be called via the 112 emergency line, however for forest fires, calling 117 will link you to the proper agency.

For people traveling with children, the Missing Child Line (116 000) is an essential contact. This service is available around the clock, connecting you with investigative authorities and giving assistance in troubling circumstances.

Porto's hospitals are well-equipped for emergencies. The primary facilities are the Hospital de São João (225 512 100) and the Hospital Santo António (222 077 500). Both hospitals provide extensive emergency care and are staffed by qualified medical experts.

There are various helplines accessible to provide mental health assistance. These programs provide discreet guidance and help, giving you someone to speak to during tough times.

Understanding these emergency contacts might make you feel safer and more prepared throughout your stay. Whether it's a medical emergency, a fire, or a request for police assistance, knowing who to contact guarantees that aid is just a phone call away.

Travel Tips for a Smooth Stay

Language Basics

Porto, where the Douro River meets the Atlantic, is a city that sings in Portuguese. This pleasant, melodious language is the city's lifeblood. While many residents speak English, particularly in tourist areas, learning a little Portuguese might make your visit much more enjoyable.

Begin with greetings. A simple "olá" (hello) or "Bom dia" (good morning) may make someone's day. When leaving, "Tchau" or "Adeus" will make a positive impression. Politeness is valued, thus "Por favor" (please) and "Obrigado" (thank you) are necessary. If you need to draw someone's attention or apologize, "Desculpe" (pardon me) is useful.

Using a few basic phrases makes it easier to navigate Porto. The term "Metro" refers to the underground, "Autocarro" to the bus, and "Comboio" to the train. If you're driving, search for "Estacionamento" to park. When hunger hits, "Pequeno almoço" translates to breakfast, "Almoço" to lunch, and "Jantar" to supper. Ordering meals becomes simpler with terms like "Pão" (bread), "Frango" (chicken), and "Peixe" (fish).

Porto's attractiveness stems from its combination of old and modern, which is mirrored in the language. You'll hear both classic terms and new slang. For example, "Fixe" denotes cool, but "Giro" indicates adorable. These tiny snippets of local slang may make your talks more real and entertaining.

While many individuals in Porto speak English, particularly among the younger generation and those in the hospitality business, learning Portuguese may open doors and hearts. It's not just about the words; it's about the relationships you form with others. So, while you meander around Porto's medieval streets, let the language lead you. Accept the cadence of Portuguese, and you'll discover that it adds a deep depth to your vacation experience.

Currency and Payment

The currency used in Porto is the Euro, which is represented by the recognizable € sign. Coins include denominations of 1, 2, 5, 10, 20, and 50 cents, as well as 1 and 2 euros. Banknotes vary in value from 5 to 500 euros, with bigger denominations being less typically used in routine transactions.

cash is usually accepted, when it comes to payments, although credit and debit cards are also popular. Visa and MasterCard are the most generally accepted, however, American Express and other cards may not be as popular. It's usually a good idea to carry some cash, particularly for smaller restaurants, local markets, and if you have any problems with card payments.

ATMs, known locally as "Multibanco," are widely distributed around the city. They provide an easy option to withdraw euros immediately from your bank account. Be aware of any costs your home bank may impose for foreign withdrawals.

To avoid these costs, it is sometimes more cost-efficient to withdraw greater sums less often.

There are various currency exchange possibilities. Banks, exchange bureaus, and even some hotels provide this service. However, it is best to avoid exchanging money at airports or hotels owing to their often low exchange rates and exorbitant costs. Instead, search for trustworthy exchange offices in the city core. Always verify the exchange rate and any extra costs before completing a transaction to guarantee you're receiving a good price.

Digital payments are growing more common in Porto. Many locations offer mobile payment methods such as Apple Purchase and Google Pay, allowing you to purchase without carrying cash or credit cards. Furthermore, prepaid travel cards may be a simple and safe method to handle your money while traveling.

Tipping in Porto is optional but appreciated for excellent service. In restaurants, it is typical to round up the bill or leave a little tip of around 5-10%. Taxi drivers often round up to the closest euro.

WiFi and Connectivity

Porto's excellent Wi-Fi infrastructure makes it easy to stay connected. The city has made tremendous steps in ensuring that both residents and tourists have easy access to the internet. Many locations provide public Wi-Fi, including parks, squares, and public buildings. The "Porto Digital" network is especially significant, having linked millions of devices and possessing a large optical fiber network1.

Cafés and restaurants often provide free Wi-Fi, making it simple to check your emails or share your most recent vacation photographs while enjoying a coffee or meal. Simply ask for the password, and you'll be online in no time. Many hotels and motels now include free Wi-Fi, so you can remain connected from the comfort of your room.

Those who want more dependable and quicker internet might consider purchasing a local SIM card. Major carriers such as

MEO, NOS, and Vodafone provide a variety of plans, including prepaid choices that are ideal for tourists. These plans often provide high data allotment, allowing you to stream, browse, and remain connected without worrying about running out of data.

Fiber-optic broadband is generally accessible, if you want to remain longer or need a more consistent connection for work, Portugal is famed for its fast internet, and Porto is no exception. You may anticipate speeds comparable to those of other major European cities, making it a good alternative for digital nomads and remote workers.

ATMs, known locally as "Multibanco," are widely distributed around the city. They provide an easy option to withdraw euros immediately from your bank account. Be aware of any costs your home bank may impose for foreign withdrawals. To avoid these costs, it is sometimes more cost-efficient to withdraw greater sums less often.

There are various currency exchange possibilities. Banks, exchange bureaus, and even some hotels provide this service. However, it is best to avoid exchanging money at airports or hotels owing to their often low exchange rates and exorbitant costs. Instead, search for trustworthy exchange offices in the city core. Always verify the exchange rate and any extra costs before completing a transaction to guarantee you're receiving a good price.

Digital payments are growing more common in Porto. Many locations offer mobile payment methods such as Apple Purchase and Google Pay, allowing you to purchase without carrying cash or credit cards. Furthermore, prepaid travel cards may be a simple and safe method to handle your money while traveling.

Tipping in Porto is optional but appreciated for excellent service. In restaurants, it is typical to round up the bill or leave a little tip of around 5-10%. Taxi drivers often round up to the closest euro.

Understanding the local currency and payment methods can help you negotiate your transactions and enjoy your stay in Porto, whether you're getting a coffee at a neighborhood café, eating at a riverfront restaurant, or shopping in one of the city's attractive shops.

Tip for Solo Travelers

Traveling alone to Porto is an experience full of charm and discovery. This city, with its rich history and lively culture, provides an ideal balance of old-world charm and contemporary amenities. Here are some suggestions to make your solo trip unique.

Begin your day with a leisurely walk along the Ribeira, the ancient riverbank region. The cobblestone lanes and colorful houses offer a lovely backdrop ideal for a morning stroll. Grab a coffee from one of the numerous cafés and watch the city come alive. The residents are welcoming and eager to tell anecdotes about their cherished city.

Porto's public transit is reliable and simple to use. The metro system is clean and secure, making it ideal for lone travelers. If you want a more picturesque journey, take one of the old trams that run through the city's small streets. Take a trip on the Gaia cable car, which provides spectacular views of the Douro River and the metropolis.

Accommodation choices are many, ranging from low-cost hostels to opulent hotels. Consider staying at a guesthouse or boutique hotel in the city center for a genuinely authentic experience. These venues generally have a more personal touch and may give valuable insights into local life.

Solo tourists are usually concerned about their safety, although Porto is typically safe and hospitable. Keep your valuables safe, particularly in congested locations, and avoid poorly lighted streets at night. It's usually a good idea to have a map or navigation software on hand, since the city's twisting lanes and steep slopes may be difficult to navigate.

The cuisine in Porto is always a highlight of every vacation. Don't miss out on eating the local delicacies, such as the famed Francesinha, a substantial sandwich that can be eaten on its own. For a sweet treat, try a pastel de nata, a delightful custard pastry popular in Portuguese cuisine. Dining alone is normal and very fine, so feel free to eat at one of the numerous restaurants or food markets.

Porto is also famed for its wine, notably port wine made in the surrounding Douro Valley. Many wine cellars provide tours and tastings, which are a terrific way to learn about the region's winemaking traditions. It is a social activity that is ideal for meeting both other visitors and locals.

Explore the majestic São Bento Railway Station, notable for its delicate azulejo tile work, or visit the world-renowned Livraria Lello bookshop. The Clérigos Tower provides panoramic views of the city, but expect a bit of a hike.

If you want to unwind, visit one of the city's numerous parks or gardens. The Crystal Palace Gardens provide a calm escape with stunning views of the river. Alternatively, take a day excursion to the local beaches to enjoy the sun and surf.

Porto's nightlife is bustling and diverse, offering something for everyone. The city comes alive after dark, with charming wine bars and bustling nightclubs. Rua Galeria de Paris and Rua Cândido dos Reis are prominent nightlife destinations, with a variety of pubs and clubs catering to all tastes.

Traveling alone in Porto is a gratifying experience that enables you to fully immerse yourself in the city's distinct environment. It's a place that will make an indelible impression because of its kind inhabitants, rich culture, and breathtaking environment.

Last Thoughts and Resources

As your trip through this colorful city draws to a close, it's evident that the memories you make here will last long after you leave. The charm of the little alleyways, the kindness of the residents, and the rich history woven into every corner combine to produce an unforgettable experience.

There are several resources accessible to people interested in learning more about the local culture. The city's tourist office is an excellent starting point, with maps, brochures, and insider information on the finest sites to visit. Local bookshops often provide a range of guidebooks that give a more detailed look at the city's history and attractions.

If you want to learn more about local food, try taking a cooking class. These lessons not only teach you how to cook traditional foods, but they also provide you with a better knowledge of the ingredients and methods that distinguish local cuisine. Many sessions are conducted by local chefs who are eager to share their expertise and love of cuisine.

For art enthusiasts, the city's museums and galleries provide a variety of resources. From modern art to historic treasures, there is something for everyone. Many museums give guided tours and courses to help visitors better comprehend the artwork and artists on exhibit.

If you want to return or just want to keep connected to the city, try joining a local club or group. These organizations often hold events and activities that enable you to remain involved with the local community while also learning about the city's culture and history.

For anyone interested in learning more about the city's culture, history, and food, there are several resources available. Whether you are a first-time visitor or a frequent tourist, there is always something new to discover and appreciate.

Conclusion

As we near the end of our tour through Porto, it becomes evident that this city is more than simply a destination; it is an experience waiting to happen. Porto welcomes you to discover its rich tapestry, from the breathtaking views along the Douro River to the bustling districts steeped in history and culture.

Whether you're sipping a drink of port wine, strolling around the vibrant Ribeira area, or admiring the exquisite azulejos that grace its buildings, each moment provides an insight into the heart of this amazing city.

Traveling around Porto fosters a greater appreciation for the basic joys of life an afternoon spent at a small café, a walk through old markets, or an unplanned encounter with a friendly local.

Allow this guide to be your companion as you discover hidden jewels and negotiate the twisting alleys, but remember to allow room for spontaneity. The unexpected often provides the basis for the finest storytelling.

Carry an exploratory attitude with you as you go on your trip to Porto. Accept the warmth of its people, the delights of its food, and the splendor of its sceneries. Porto awaits, eager to include you in its story so go out, investigate, and let the city leave an unforgettable stamp on your heart. Safe travels!

Scan the QRCODE to view full Porto map

Printed in Dunstable, United Kingdom